WITHOUT WAVERING

RESILIENT FAITH BUILT
ON THE PROMISES OF GOD

ALEXANDRA HOOVER

Lifeway Press®
Brentwood, Tennessee

ISBN: 978-1-0877-7937-9
Item: 005841093
Dewey decimal classification: 234.2
Subject headings: HOPE \ FAITH \ WOMEN

To order additional copies of this resource, write Lifeway Resources Customer Service; 200 Powell Place, Suite 100, Brentwood, TN 37027-7707; FAX order to 615.251.5933; call toll-free 800.458.2772; email orderentry@lifeway.com; or order online at lifeway.com.

Printed in the United States of America

Lifeway Women Bible Studies
Lifeway Resources
200 Powell Place, Suite 100,
Brentwood, TN 37027-7707

EDITORIAL TEAM,
LIFEWAY WOMEN
BIBLE STUDIES

Becky Loyd
Director, Lifeway Women

Tina Boesch
Manager

Chelsea Waack
Production Leader

Laura Magness
Content Editor

Erin Franklin
Production Editor

Lauren Ervin
Graphic Designer

CONTENTS

how to use this study

PERSONAL STUDY Each week you'll have five days of personal study with the last day as a reflection day. After you finish a week, be sure to watch the video. The first session is video only.

VIDEO VIEWER GUIDE Each session of *Without Wavering* ends with a teaching video from Alexandra. The Viewer Guide page provides you with a place to take notes from the video teachings and from your small group discussion time. You'll want to begin your study by watching the Session One video and taking notes on page 10.

VIDEO ACCESS With the purchase of this book, you have access to videos from Alexandra that provide insight to help you better understand and apply what you study. **You'll find detailed information on how to access the teaching videos on the card inserted in the back of your Bible study book.**

LEADING A GROUP? A free leader guide PDF is available for download at **lifeway.com/withoutwavering**. The leader guide offers several tips and helps along with discussion guides for each week.

A NOTE ABOUT BIBLE TRANSLATIONS This Bible study pulls from a variety of Bible translations, the primary one being the New International Version (NIV). All other translations will be marked by their abbreviations. You can read from any of these translations and more at biblegateway.com or on a Bible app. The names of the Bible books will be abbreviated when referenced in parentheses in this study. For a complete list of book abbreviations, download the chart available at **lifeway.com/withoutwavering**.

ALEXANDRA HOOVER is a wife, mother of three, daughter, Bible teacher, speaker, and bestselling author of *Eyes Up: How to Trust God's Heart by Tracing His Hand*. She's passionate about communicating the gospel's beauty and hope, whether through writing or speaking, online or in person. She aims for her words to spur people on to two things—knowing who God is and knowing who they are in Him. Alexandra has the privilege of serving on staff at Transformation Church and spends her days loving on her family, dancing with her kids, and living on mission right where God has her.

A WORD FROM THE AUTHOR

Dear friend, I'm so glad you're here. No matter how you arrived, or who handed you this study, or what made you say yes, what matters is that you're here, and that is no mistake.

The concept of faith used to feel mythical, almost fictitious, to me. Like a concept you'd hear about in your favorite fairytale. Before I knew Jesus, it felt more like a make-believe disposition. *Just have faith; God's in control.* I'm sure you've heard that before. Once I became a follower of Jesus, I knew faith was about something more, something deeper, but it was still so difficult for me to grasp.

Blind faith is the term that played over and over in my mind as I took steps to know and trust God. I've not always been the most trusting person; people have let me down so many times that it's hard to put my trust in anyone else. The thought of blind faith felt absolutely too costly and too terrifying. I struggled to have faith and trust in God even though I knew Him to be good. Maybe you can relate.

When the storms of life—and there are many—knock you down, and you look up from the ground to find yourself in a world of disarray, perhaps the words *I just can't keep doing this* rise up in you. What happens when the prayer goes unanswered? When your soul is so worn that the thought of getting back into the deep blue sea of life feels impossible? You know it's only a matter of time before those waves crash again. What holds you up when everything else has let you down? The only sustaining answer is this: *You hold onto the faith and hope you have in Jesus.*

I'm not sure what season of life you're in or what your relationship with Jesus looks like today, but learning how to look to Him, to stay resiliently focused on Him, is what this study is all about. We'll begin with the question, *What actually is faith?* And then we'll consider how we build up a resilient faith, one that's unwavering regardless of our circumstances or challenges. How can we be women who live from this firm foundation in certainty and confidence?

When I began writing this study, I thought about you, the woman who, whether experienced in the faith or just getting started, needs a firm anchor and framework of a strong faith to work from.

The heart of the study is beautifully encompassed in Hebrews 10:23 (CSB),

> Let us hold on to the confession of our hope without wavering, since he who promised is faithful.

Throughout this Bible study, we'll spend a lot of time studying Hebrews 10–12 and the writer's many examples of unwavering faith. We'll also consider the early church, Paul, and concepts like spiritual rhythms and God's promise-keeping nature to help us understand what faith in action looks like.

When we truly believe that He who promised is faithful, then we can respond with a faith that is built up with resilience and perseverance, a faith without wavering because we know that God is going to finish His good work (Phil. 1:6). My hope and prayer for you in this study is that you walk away with key principles, truths, and promises to help form your faith, strengthen your relationship with Jesus, and equip you for this beautiful life we've been given to steward.

THIS IS FOR YOU

For tired eyes that seek perseverance.
For learning to love ourselves as God loves us.
For embracing this season and all its nuance.
For calling out courage and bravery.
For learning to serve without applause.
For learning to keep a steady gaze on Jesus.
For hope and peace.
For learning to pick ourselves back up.
For being honest and vulnerable about our lack.
For the gift of embracing each new battle scar.
For allowing God to hold us and grace to carry us.
For layers being pulled back so that new things can become.
For a faith without wavering, found only in Christ.

– *Alexandra*

Introduction
THIS IS FOR YOU

Session One
Video Viewer Guide
THIS IS FOR YOU

WATCH the Session One video and take notes below.

GROUP DISCUSSION / QUESTIONS FOR REFLECTION

A leader guide is available for download at lifeway.com/withoutwavering

1. If you were to attempt to define faith in God, especially to someone who doesn't have a relationship with Him, how would you explain it?

2. What is one word you would use to describe the current state of your relationship with God?

3. Read the "This Is for You" manifesto (p. 7). Which of these statements resonate with you as you begin this study?

4. What are some hindrances, distractions, or obstacles you might face in being able to complete the personal study each week? If you're a Bible study veteran, what tips would you offer on how to stay the course in our study?

5. What is one way you want to ask God to work in you through this study?

TO ACCESS THE VIDEO TEACHING SESSIONS, USE THE
INSTRUCTIONS IN THE BACK OF YOUR BIBLE STUDY BOOK.

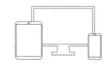

LET US HOLD ON
TO THE CONFESSION
OF OUR HOPE
WITHOUT
WAVERING,
SINCE HE
WHO PROMISED
IS FAITHFUL.

HEBREWS 10:23 (CSB)

The Key to
UNWAVERING
FAITH

What is *faith*, let alone a faith that is "without wavering" (Heb. 10:23, CSB)? This is where we begin our study. In this week's session, we'll not only become familiar with the definition of *faith*, but we'll also begin to wrestle with what it means for followers of Jesus to truly live *by faith*. We'll spend our time in Hebrews 11 and the list of Bible figures whose examples help us understand what faith looked like for them. Most importantly, we're reminded that Jesus— the promised One hinted at throughout the Old Testament—is the One on whom our faith and hope ultimately rests. What we'll read this week is inspiring, and I hope it encourages you as much as it's encouraged me.

SESSION 02 MEMORY VERSES

The LORD makes firm the steps of the one who delights in him; though he may stumble, he will not fall, for the LORD upholds him with his hand.

PSALM 37:23-24

WHAT WE MEAN WHEN WE TALK *about Faith*

I didn't grow up a church girl, or a faith girl, or a God girl. I guess you can say that I knew of God—I'd heard other people talk about Him—but that was it. Every summer as a little girl I traveled to Venezuela to stay with an aunt and uncle. I looked forward to it every year; it was a time to go back to my other home. Rest and peace awaited. One particular summer, though, was notably different. I was around thirteen or fourteen and was a deeply inquisitive teenager with lots of questions about life—and God.

My cousin attended a private Catholic school with a community of people who also attended the Catholic church just down the road from my aunt and uncle's home. That summer I spent more time in a church than ever before. My cousin was attending classes for her confirmation, which is one of the seven sacraments of the Roman Catholic faith and one of the steps to becoming a part of the Roman Catholic Church. And so, I tagged along to many of her classes.

The priest seemed like the right person to take my questions to, so that's exactly what I did! First item on my list to address? The creation account. I know, super light conversation. My following questions surrounding doubt, suffering, and the circumstances of life challenged every word that came out of his mouth. *What if God isn't the God over all? What if He isn't kind or good? What if Jesus didn't rise from the dead?* My brown hair and hands moved all around as I questioned his beliefs and faith.

Instead of dismissing me or explaining God away, the priest welcomed my curiosity. He smiled and smirked, willing to listen to a young girl who was taking her first steps toward a relationship with God. That is the summer when my journey toward Jesus began, and it's been a wild ride ever since.

What do you consider to be the beginning of your faith journey, like my summer in Venezuela? What questions do you remember having, and who played an important role in that moment or season?

FAITH DEFINED

This is a Bible study about building a resilient, sturdy faith in God, so I want to make sure we begin with a solid understanding of what we mean when we talk about "faith."

Look up FAITH in an online dictionary. List the top two definitions that show up.

1.

2.

READ HEBREWS 11:1-3. Write down the description of faith given in verse 1.

How does this description of faith compare with what you found online?

I mentioned in the introduction that we will spend a lot of time in Hebrews 10–12. That's because these chapters contain valuable insight into how God wants us to understand a life of faith in Him. The book of Hebrews defines faith as "the reality [or assurance] of what is hoped for, the proof [or conviction] of what is not seen" (11:1, CSB). (For more on this, check out the Further Study on p. 21.) Here's an explanation of this verse that I find helpful:

> Faith is not merely holding to certain teachings, such as that God exists, but rather it is a strong conviction that the world around us is part of a greater plan, God's plan. Faith means that although at times the world looks chaotic and uncontrolled, we feel deep down that this chaotic world is not where we truly live. Rather, our existences are guided by God's strength and power.[1]

The description of faith in Hebrews 11:1 is part of a wider theme in Hebrews—an invitation to see how the things in the world around us are best understood through the bigger picture of God's story, a story that began with creation and culminates in Jesus. In fact, this is where the whole book begins.

READ HEBREWS 1:1-3a, **printed below. As you read the verses, circle each word that describes who Jesus (the "Son") is. Underline each word or phrase that describes what Jesus does or has done.**

Long ago, at many times and in many ways, God spoke to our fathers by the prophets, but in these last days he has spoken to us by his Son, whom he appointed the heir of all things, through whom also he created the world. He is the radiance of the glory of God and the exact imprint of his nature, and he upholds the universe by the word of his power.
HEBREWS 1:1-3a (ESV)

OUR FAITH IS THE REALITY OF OUR HOPE IN CHRIST.

It's all about Jesus! He is the One we latch our faith and hope onto. The New Testament suggests that faith and hope go hand in hand for the follower of Jesus. Our faith is the reality of our hope in Christ; it's "the *proof* that what we believe is *real*, as well as the *certainty* that our *hopes* will become actualized in heaven."[2] The heartbeat to the book of Hebrews is having a faith anchored and built up in Christ and Christ alone.

READ BACK OVER HEBREWS 11:1-3 ONE MORE TIME. Now I want you to write your own definition of faith, keeping in mind what you've studied today. How would you define it to someone who has no religious upbringing, like teenager me?

When I think about the definition of *faith*, it's like the foundation of a sturdy house or the active ingredient that makes the recipe work. It's the quiet yet bold something that whispers hope and light in the midst of so much dark. Faith is what moves us to believe and to see, even when we can't make sense of it. It's like the breeze you feel on a spring day or the oxygen we inhale with every breath. We can't see it, but it's there.

> *FAITH IS WHAT MOVES US TO BELIEVE AND TO SEE, EVEN WHEN WE CAN'T MAKE SENSE OF IT.*

When I read Hebrews 11:1-3, I see an invitation to live out my faith based on the reality of the hope I have that Jesus lived and died for me, that He conquered death so I can spend eternity with Him, and that He will do as He said and return and right all wrongs. This is the good news, the gospel, Jesus's life, death, and resurrection as the sacrifice and atonement for all our sins (Rom. 1:3-4). Jesus is the Perfecter, the One who was, and is, and is to come (Rev. 1:4).

As we walk through the rest of this study together, may we remember that our faith is a gift! God is the Creator and Giver of it (Eph. 2:8-10). We don't have to will our way to a more resilient faith; we couldn't if we tried. One key to an unwavering faith in Jesus is surrendering each day, each moment, to Him. It's believing in His promises and allowing Him to use you for the good works He has planned.

Before you close today, spend time in prayer. Thank God for the gift that is your faith and for Jesus, the One in whom your faith is secure. Ask God to spend these next six sessions strengthening your faith in Him.

FURTHER STUDY

Read the Bible for long and you'll realize the term *faith* is used many times (more than two hundred in the New Testament alone!). With this many uses, it can be hard to wrap our minds around a clear understanding of what this concept means for the Christian. The following description from the *Holman Bible Dictionary* helps us lay a good foundation for what we mean when we talk about faith.

"The Greek noun, *pistis* (faith), is related to the verb *pisteuo* (I have faith, trust, believe). . . . In the New Testament faith is used in a number of ways, but primarily with the meaning 'trust' or 'confidence' in God. Mark 1:15 introduces and summarizes the Gospel with Jesus' charge to his hearers to 'repent . . . and believe the gospel.' (The word usually translated 'believe' in this verse is the verb form of 'faith' for which there is no English equivalent. The call is repeated as 'Have faith in God'; using the noun form, in Mark 11:22.) Thus, Jesus called His hearers to place their confidence in God."[3] Outside the Gospels, faith is used in a variety of ways, all of which point back to that main understanding. Here are a few of them:

- sanctification (Acts 26:18);

- purification (Acts 15:9);

- justification or imputed righteousness (Rom. 4:5; 5:1; Gal. 3:24);

- adoption as children of God (Gal. 3:26);

- a fruit of the Holy Spirit (Gal. 5:22)—something God creates in a person;

- the state of salvation (Eph. 2:8-9).

"Each of these comes by faith. As in the Gospels, faith is an attitude toward and relationship with God mediated by Christ Jesus. It is surrender to God's gift of righteousness in Christ rather than seeking to achieve righteousness alone."[4] The Bible never directly defines faith, but it comes close in Hebrews 11:1, "Now faith is the reality of what is hoped for, the proof of what is not seen."

"Hebrews closely ties faith . . . to Christian hope. The personal conviction of faith encourages the Christian to continue hoping for the fulfillment of the promises of God . . . The 'things hoped for' have a reality greater than anyone's hoping for them. Faith is then meant as a sort of foretaste of the hoped for things."[5] The writer of Hebrews uses this word to speak to loyalty, allegiance, a following of God no matter what.

By Faith

GOD'S STRENGTH IN ME

When I was a girl, I remember walking down the halls of my middle school and hoping that no one would see just how scared I was to be there. I was being severely bullied by a group of girls who made it their goal in life to convince me I wasn't welcome and to try to get me to just give up.

Each day I walked in with that feeling in the pit of my stomach—you know which one I'm talking about, the one that rears its atrocious head when insecurities, doubt, and worry begin to make themselves a home in your heart and mind. This feeling became a posture of self-doubt, fear, and angst. And tragically, it's never gone away; I've just adapted to it. Life has a way of awakening the insecurities that lay dormant.

It didn't take long before I struggled to keep showing up in a space that left me wounded. But do you know what helped me keep going? My middle school counselor, Mrs. Polard. She was a soft place to land, a woman of love and light for a heart that needed it. With her I was able to laugh-cry off the days that crippled me with fear and sadness. I trusted her. And so, I showed up.

I tell you this story because it reminds me of our journeys through life. If your life looks anything like mine, then every day there are moments we come up against, each one with the potential to wound us, to steal our joy. We live in a fallen world marred by sin. What hope can we cling to? We need something—Someone—to look to, Someone to help pull us through. Being a Jesus follower invites us to something greater, something more than the brokenness of our world. In Christ we find belonging and purpose, for today and forever. In Christ we receive the resilience to show up and step forward.

Yesterday, we considered what faith is, using Hebrews 11:1-3 as our guide. Today, we'll pick up where we left off in Hebrews 11. After defining faith, verses 4-38 give us example after example of people in the Old Testament who—"by faith"—walked in obedience to God and lived out their God-given assignments as His children. Their stories show they were not always without fear or doubt but that they had trust in their God.

READ HEBREWS 11:4-12 AND FILL IN THE CHART THAT FOLLOWS.

PASSAGE	PERSON	ACT OF FAITH
Verse 4		
Verses 5-6		
Verse 7		
Verses 8-10		
Verses 11-12		

What stands out to you as you reflect on the examples of faith you just read?

The examples we see in verses 4-12—Abel, Enoch, Noah, Abraham, and Sarah—take us back to the earliest chapters of Genesis. From the moment Adam and Eve were banished from the garden and the presence of God, His relationship with His children became one of faith rather than sight. *By faith . . . By faith . . . By faith.* This phrase is the heartbeat of Hebrews 11 and the key to how each of these individuals lived in obedience to God, even as they faced hardships like ridicule, isolation, barrenness, and other all-too-familiar trials.

Earlier in the book of Hebrews, the author encouraged his readers "to persevere in the face of adversity, and have confidence in God, assuring them that His promises will be fulfilled (Heb. 10:19-38)," a theme he'll return to again in chapter 12.[6] Our friends in Hebrews 11 were motivated by faith because of who they knew God to be and the power of His strength at work in them. This is the key to faith in action, to a life where our weakness does not keep us from showing up but is made perfect in God's strength.

Think about a time recently when you tried to work through a challenging situation in your own strength. How did operating from your strength hinder growth in your faith?

On the other hand, how does relying on God's strength help you build up an unwavering faith?

That last question is harder to answer, isn't it? I love the way the apostle Paul helps us here:

> Therefore, so that I would not exalt myself, a thorn in the flesh was given to me, a messenger of Satan to torment me so that I would not exalt myself. Concerning this, I pleaded with the Lord three times that it would leave me. But he said to me, "My grace is sufficient for you, for my power is perfected in weakness."
>
> *Therefore, I will most gladly boast all the more about my weaknesses, so that Christ's power may reside in me.* So I take pleasure in weaknesses, insults, hardships, persecutions, and in difficulties, for the sake of Christ. For when I am weak, then I am strong.
>
> 2 CORINTHIANS 12:7b-10 (CSB, EMPHASIS ADDED)

When we are left with nothing, we boast in our weaknesses. When we can't keep going, we boast in our weaknesses. When life is too much for us to handle, we boast in our weaknesses. When God calls us to move through life, we live from His power and not ours because faith in Him is our anchor. Self-preservation will never get us where surrender can. I hope it's great news for you to hear that you don't have to muster up the emotional grit to take on the pain in your life; you can hand it over to Jesus—Someone much more capable than you are to carry you through.

As a wife, mother, daughter, and friend, I still have days where I feel like that little girl walking the halls of my middle school. I've spent nights collecting tears of emotional and spiritual exhaustion on my pillow, hiding away from the world as if my weaknesses and weary soul were things to be hidden. But it's in moments when obstacles do come— when the winds take us down, when the waves crash over us—that I'm learning to rely on God, His power, and His strength. While He may not immediately and miraculously change my difficult circumstances, I do know He will give me the power to face whatever is in front of me at the moment. I've seen Him do so time and again in my life and in the pages of His Word.

Reflect on the past week. What is one "by faith" moment you've had this week? Write it in the space below, then spend some time talking to God. Specifically ask Him to help you live by faith more in the coming days.

BY FAITH I . . .

day 03

By Faith
EVEN IN THE HARD THINGS

I've always wanted to see wild horses in person, the ones that seem to run with unrelenting courage and strength. Leaving behind whatever was, and only seeing what is ahead. I don't remember the exact movie where I first saw wild horses, but there's a scene where a woman meets these beautiful creatures, and in that moment, she begins to see life again. They sparked something in her. Maybe it was the courage to go again, the courage to get back up, to move forward, onward. (If you know the name of the movie, make sure to let me know!) As I watched her choose hope again, as I saw this resilience and gentle but fierce zeal rise up, my soul resonated with it. I wanted this.

These horses make me think of the faith we see on display in Hebrews 11. A faith fueled by trust—running the race ahead well, knowing we are being guided by a God who is trustworthy and good, and keeping our eyes on the "better place" that awaits us. Yesterday, we saw examples of this unwavering faith from the lives of Abel, Enoch, Noah, Abraham, and Sarah (Heb. 11:4-16). Today we're going to jump back into Hebrews 11 and the "by faith" encouragement held there. Let's pick up where we left off.

READ HEBREWS 11:17-31 and fill in the chart, just like yesterday!

PASSAGE	PERSON	ACT OF FAITH
Verses 17-19		
Verse 20		
Verse 21		
Verse 22		
Verse 23		

PASSAGE	PERSON	ACT OF FAITH
Verses 24–26		
Verse 27		
Verse 28		
Verse 29		

What thoughts do you have as you reflect on the examples of faith you just read?

Which example encourages you the most in your current season of life or a trial you're walking through today? Put a star next to it on the chart.

Like the examples we looked at yesterday, this list of "by faith" moments continues with more examples—including Abraham (whom we'll look at more closely later in our study) and on through the rest of the patriarchs, Moses, the exodus out of Egypt, and Joshua's conquest of the promised land. Most surprising in this list is the example of Rahab, a non-Israelite (Gentile) and a prostitute, who had faith in God because of His power and glory on display through the exodus events. The common thread through all these examples is trust in the Lord that motivates action.

NOW READ HEBREWS 11:32-38. **The people in Hebrews 11 are often referred to as "heroes of the faith." What do you learn about being heroic in God's eyes from their examples and what's written about them in verses 32-38?**

How does that compare with the way you usually think about people who are worth imitating? What perspective does this give you on your current trials?

We typically think of heroes as the strongest, most beautiful, richest, most powerful, and so on—they are the best and most capable among us, and they are the ones doing the rescuing. But when we read through Hebrews 11, we're reminded the "heroes" of faithfulness are far from perfect, their lives were far from easy, and they needed a Rescuer. They were like you and me, people living life on mission in the mundane. But we get to see the fruit of their choosing obedience and faithfulness. Just as Jesus called them to faithfulness, so He calls us to a life of faithfulness in Him. Although that life is often costly and it comes with its own set of sacrifices, the reward far outweighs the cost.

> I have told you these things so that in me you may
> have peace. You will have suffering in this world.
> Be courageous! I have conquered the world.
>
> JOHN 16:33 (CSB)

May this be our resolve, our faith in action, too. Our faith will take us where our sight can't. When we trust the will of God, we will follow the plan of God by walking out our obedience—loving Him and His people.

> The LORD makes firm the steps of the one who
> delights in him; though he may stumble, he will
> not fall, for the LORD upholds him with his hand.
>
> PSALM 37:23-24

What is a specific situation or an area of your life where God is asking you to trust Him more? Think of at least one example and write it down. Then, use that as the basis of your prayer time as you wrap up today's study.

By Faith in Jesus
THE PROMISE

I try to not break promises, but of course there are times when I do. I've been known to be the person who can't tell people no, so there are times when I overcommit myself, knowing good and well that I won't be able to follow through. A few years back, my son Kingston got the short end of my well-meaning broken promise.

I promised Kingston I would take him out on a mommy/son date, and I'd been repeating that same promise for several weeks. But I was absolutely exhausted from the season of life we were in, and as each evening came and went, I kept reassuring Kingston this date would happen soon. I lacked the courage to honestly say, "Mommy just can't right now. Let's try and find another way to connect until these next two weeks settle down." I didn't say that, and I ended up letting him down.

I've also experienced moments and people much like myself who have promised me the world, only to come back with empty dreams and unmet expectations. Have you ever experienced this? I'm sure you have! Promises are so misused that I think we've lost touch of the integrity, the weightiness, of what a promise holds.

> **Reflect on the last promise you broke. What happened, and how do you feel thinking back on that?**

> **Now think about the last time someone broke a promise they made to you. How did you feel at the time, and how was your relationship with that person affected?**

Before we look at the last two verses of Hebrews 11, I want you to spend a few minutes considering God's promise-keeping nature. (For an even longer list, check out the article "What are the promises of God?" at gotquestions.org.)

- "God promised to bless Abraham and, through his descendants, the whole world (Genesis 12:2-3). This promise, called the Abrahamic Covenant, pointed to the coming Messiah for whom Abraham looked (John 8:56).

- God promised that all things will work out for good for His children (Romans 8:28). This is the broader picture that keeps us from being dismayed by present circumstances.

- God promised comfort in our trials (2 Corinthians 1:3-4). He has a plan, and one day we will be able to share the comfort we receive.

- God promised new life in Christ (2 Corinthians 5:17). Salvation is the beginning of a brand-new existence.

- God promised every spiritual blessing in Christ (Ephesians 1:3).

- God promised to finish the work He started in us (Philippians 1:6). God does nothing in half measures. He started the work of redemption in us, and He will be sure to complete it.

- God promised peace when we pray (Philippians 4:6-7). His peace is protection. It 'will guard your hearts and your minds in Christ.'"

- God promised to supply our needs (Matthew 6:33; Philippians 4:19). . . . We are more valuable than the birds, and our heavenly Father feeds them (Matthew 6:26)."[7]

   Take a few moments to reflect on these promises. Which ones speak most to you today and why?

   In general, what do these promises teach you about God? How do they strengthen your faith in Him?

In Hebrews 11:39-40 (CSB) we read,

> All these were approved through their faith, but
> they did not receive what was promised, since
> God had provided something better for us, so that
> they would not be made perfect without us.

What do you think the writer meant by "what was promised" and "something better for us"?

NOW READ HEBREWS 6:17-20 AND HEBREWS 12:1-2. How do these passages help you better understand God's love and faithful promise toward you?

Earlier this week, we considered the example of Abraham, and how, as he followed God, he lived a life of faith in action. We first see God in Genesis 17:4 promise Abraham that he would be a father of many nations, a promise God was faithful to keep as He grew His people from Abraham's family line, which is the focus of the rest of the book of Genesis. Ultimately though, this promise was to be fulfilled in Christ Jesus, because through Him, acceptance into God's family became available to everyone, regardless of lineage. Jesus is the answer to the promise the Old Testament saints kept their eyes on, and He is the "something better" available to us.

GOD IS FAITHFUL TO KEEP ALL HIS PROMISES.

READ JOHN 3:16 and write it here:

God is not like us; He doesn't overcommit or fail us. He doesn't overextend love; He freely gives it, never running out. And He is faithful to keep all His promises (Ps. 145:13). Jesus is our assurance of that, and He is the One on whom an unwavering faith is built. Because without Him, we have nothing.

The friends in Hebrews 11:3-38, those who by faith obeyed God, did not get to experience the salvation available by grace through faith in Jesus. Rather, they believed God would be faithful to His promise and eagerly awaited its fulfillment. You and I today, though, get to experience this promise of salvation! And while we also eagerly wait for the day when the world will be made right, we hold fast to the promise of Jesus's return (Matt. 24:27-31; Acts 1:11; Rev. 19–20).

Resilience is built in seasons much like the people in Hebrews 11 experienced, in our times of spiritual desperation. Life can be unpredictable and full of moments when we miss God working out His promise right in front of us. But He is always at work building up our faith and transforming us into His image. Don't miss the miracle in the middle, the in-between. And remember that, unlike our Old Testament friends, we get to live in the beautiful reality of relationship with Jesus today.

READ BACK OVER JOHN 3:16. **Write down a few thoughts of reflection you have as you let your mind dwell on the truth of the gospel.**

Reflection

It's your first reflection day, dear friend. Every fifth day of study has been set aside as an intentional time for you to look back at the week. I'm giving you three questions to help focus your reflection time as well as some things to think about while you spend extra time talking to God in prayer. No matter where you are in your own journey of faith— just beginning, struggling with doubt, reminding yourself that God is faithful, years down the road of your story, or some combination of these—today's the day to process what God is showing you. Put it down on paper and meet with Him in prayer.

1. Write an explanation of "faith" in your own words, looking back at your notes from this week of study as you need to. This practice will help faith move from a general religious term to a part of your life you're able to share confidently with others.

2. What is one big takeaway or main idea you want to remember from this week of study?

3. What is one idea or thought you need to lay down that contradicts God's faithful love for you?

4. Now write out an honest prayer reflecting on the current season of your faith and what Jesus is teaching you. Use the space here or a separate journal so you can look back on this prayer when you need it later.

WATCH the Session Two video and take notes below.

GROUP DISCUSSION / QUESTIONS FOR REFLECTION

A leader guide is available for download at lifeway.com/withoutwavering

1. What day of personal study had the most impact on you? Why?

2. How did what you heard on the video teaching clarify, reinforce, or give new insight into what you studied this session?

3. Pick an example of faith in God from Hebrews 11 that stood out to you and share your thoughts. You might also want to share the definitions of faith you wrote down on page 33.

4. In the video, Alexandra encouraged us that a big part of faith is admitting to God that we need Him and we trust Him. Why is this hard to do? What are some lies we believe from the world that make us think surrender and neediness aren't OK?

5. Discuss your responses to the reflection questions on page 33.

TO ACCESS THE VIDEO TEACHING SESSIONS, USE THE
INSTRUCTIONS IN THE BACK OF YOUR BIBLE STUDY BOOK.

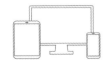

ONE KEY TO AN
UNWAVERING
FAITH IN JESUS IS
SURRENDERING EACH
DAY, EACH MOMENT,
TO HIM.

Faith in the HARD PLACES

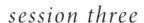

The hard places come for all of us. That's one of the saddest and most difficult aspects of life on this side of heaven, and it can be one of the biggest hurdles to unwavering faith. This is why we're talking about the hard stuff right up front. Before we go any further, I need to encourage you that the valley won't always be your home. Your faith won't always feel frail. You won't always feel like there's no end in sight. You won't always lack the confidence to love, to heal, to show up, or to keep going.

Here's what I hope you take away from this week: In the moments when you do feel frail, let God draw you closer to Him. He's reaching out a hand for you to hold onto. Let Him pick you back up. Keep your faith and hope focused on Him. I am living proof that God strengthens us to endure, corrects us through discipline, pushes us toward holiness, and picks us back up time and time again.

SESSION 03 MEMORY VERSES

Consider it a great joy, my brothers and sisters, whenever you experience various trials, because you know that the testing of your faith produces endurance.

JAMES 1:2-3 (CSB)

RUNNING THE RACE
of Endurance

I absolutely love to run, and I have since I was a teenager. I still find extreme joy and contentment when my feet hit the pavement, and I love the way my body feels as I move in one direction, my mind clear and set on where I'm headed. For years I only exercised outside. The smell of freshly cut grass, the trees telling a story of seasons changing, birds, and even the bugs I traveled with all helped keep my mind off the noise inside it. The more I ran, the more I became fixated on beating my previous time. I was getting faster, but I was also losing the art of building up stamina, endurance, and even the gift found in slowing down.

One day, as I watched the timer approach the ten-minute mark, I began to speed up my pace. But suddenly I felt led to slow down, to breathe. I thought, maybe today I'll add an incline. Maybe I can get better results for both my mind and body. And you know what, it worked! I learned inclines work your body more holistically and engage muscles that aren't moved on a fast run, and the mind catches a break, too. As I walked to my car, I felt the Lord tell me, *Alexandra, it's not always about how fast you're going but about the strength and endurance you're building up. Much like your faith.*

In your own words, without googling it or reading ahead, how would you define *endurance***?**

Merriam-Webster defines endurance as: 1: "the ability to withstand hardship or adversity, especially the ability to sustain a prolonged stressful effort or activity"; and 2: "the act or an instance of enduring or suffering."[1] When it comes to our faith, we're called to run the race of life—which is definitely a marathon and not a sprint—with endurance. But how do we get there? How do we learn to be patient in the hard places, instead of trying to sprint through them? And how do we avoid turning our backs on the Lord when things are just too hard? Our friend, the writer of Hebrews, has some helpful insight for us.

READ HEBREWS 12:1-3, where we left off last week. Write down any words or phrases that help you know what endurance looks like for the follower of Jesus.

Hebrews 11 gave us a list of Old Testament figures who displayed courage, confidence, and endurance in their faithfulness to God. These were remarkable men and women who left behind a great testament to God's faithfulness and enduring love. Hebrews 12:1 describes these people as a "cloud of witnesses" for us, a representation of God's faithfulness to His people and their faithfulness to Him.

As we look back and remember them, we also look forward, "fixing our eyes on Jesus" (v. 2). With the faithful saints behind us and Jesus before us, we're spurred on to endure life in this broken, temporary world and to fulfill the mission God has given us to love Him and love others (Matt. 22:37-39).

REREAD HEBREWS 12:2-3. In your own words, summarize what these verses say about Jesus.

Why is *considering* Jesus the key to an enduring, unwavering faith in the hard places? (See v. 3.)

The writer of Hebrews describes Jesus as "the pioneer and perfecter of faith" (v. 2). In the New Living Translation of the Bible, this description reads: "the champion who initiates and perfects our faith." Read that again—"the champion who initiates *and* perfects our faith" (emphasis added). Jesus is both the ultimate model of faithfulness for us, as well as the One in whom we place our faith. When we "consider him," as verse 3 calls us to do, we're able to view the trials of today in light of the finish line—eternity spent with Him.

If you're anything like me, it's much easier to live out my faith and to keep my eyes fixed on Jesus during the high moments than it is during the low (sometimes very low) times.

But James, in his New Testament letter, reminds us that God uses every hard thing we go through to draw us closer to Him.

LOOK UP JAMES 1:2-4 IN YOUR BIBLE. Circle or write down every word/phrase that speaks to the ways God uses our trials to shape us.

"Pure joy," "perseverance," and "mature and complete" (I'm using the NIV translation) stand out to me when I read over those verses. God uses the hard places to strengthen our faith in Him and bring us to spiritual maturity. When our backs are up against a wall, when we feel like giving up, yet we are able to keep our eyes fixed on Jesus— those are the moments when God reminds us who He is to us.

Hebrews 12:1-3 encourages us to let our faith in God and our eyes fixed on Jesus be what pushes us through the hard places. As we look at building up our faith, we throw off all sin that hinders us and aim to live a life honoring to God. Whatever weight we're carrying, we look up and remember the work of Christ, and we look around at the ones who have gone before us. These give us the motivation to run well the race of endurance in the faith. The marathon is long, and we will encounter turbulence and trials along the way, but in the end, Jesus will be there to meet us. Let's keep our gaze fixed on Him!

Is God calling you to endurance in a specific hard place today? How does what you've read encourage your faith?

You have a role to play in being part of this "great cloud of witnesses" for other Christ followers (Heb. 12:1). What is one way you can do that this week? Who is one person you can encourage through your own example of faithfulness?

SOMETIMES IT'S
Discipline

I have a difficult time trusting people, and for a long time, I didn't even know it. Had we met just a few years ago, I would've told you I'm a generally trusting person. And yet, I found myself questioning the motives of most around me, wondering if their intent was good. I brought up this layer of conflict I was feeling to my counselor with honest curiosity. "I just realized that I don't seem to trust the intent of most people." She asked, "Well, what do you believe about God's intent for you as your Father?"

I paused, tears welling up in my eyes and the knot in my throat closing in. I looked around the room anxiously trying to avoid eye contact with her. All I could think about was my dad, my earthly father, and all the letdowns I experienced with him. And although I knew in my head that God's character wasn't my dad's, the hurt and wounds left enough of a sting that even years later, most of how I viewed life was through that lens.

I believe that our earthly relationships inform how we see God, more than the other way around. We easily see God as we see people, who are often unreliable, not trustworthy, and unfaithful. How on earth is our faith to be founded in God if we believe Him to be like every person who has disappointed us?

> Sit quietly with God for a moment and ask Him to prepare your heart for what He wants to teach you today.

A GOD WHO CARES

Having encouraged endurance in the faith (Heb. 12:1-3), the writer of Hebrews next invites us to know God as Father, as the One who not only comforts our wounds but cares for them. A Father who guides His children, disciplines when needed, and has our best intentions at hand.

Unfortunately, many of us struggle to believe those things are true about God, don't we? Even if you've had a wonderful relationship with your earthly father, he will have let you down from time to time just by nature of him being a fellow sinner in this long, hard journey alongside you. Regardless of the personal experience you bring to the table here, we all have a tendency to lump God in with the world.

> READ HEBREWS 12:4-11, with a focus on God as Father. Write down one or two sections that speak to you about the character and heart of God the Father.

The original recipients of the letter of Hebrews are believed to have been first-century Jewish Christians. Because of the rampant persecution of Christians during the growth of the early church, Jewish Christians in particular were in danger of turning their backs on their faith and resorting to their Jewish traditions and rules. So here, the writer of Hebrews reminds them that God is their good Father, and everything they faced—from persecution for following Jesus to discipline for personal sin—they faced as His dearly loved children.[2]

I often talk about a belief system that kept me hostage to doubt and fear for quite some time and occasionally still tries to rear its ugly head: "God may be good, just not to me." The sheer volume of suffering and difficulties in my life meant the character of God was consistently in question. If this is you, hear this from me today: God is good. He sees you, He knows you, and He cares about you.

GOD IS GOOD. HE SEES YOU, HE KNOWS YOU, AND HE CARES ABOUT YOU.

Whenever you doubt this, just look to Jesus, the clearest reflection of the goodness of our heavenly Father.

> Taste and see that the LORD is good; blessed
> is the one who takes refuge in him.
>
> PSALM 34:8

Believing that our Father cares—that His intent is good—not only helps us see God for who He is; it also helps to tear down the walls of distrust and unbelief that we've placed God behind. Understanding God as our Father establishes trust and peace within us. When we see God as a good Father, we trust Him not only with our dreams, desires, and prayers but also with our transformation.

What is one way you've assigned a trait of the world to God recently that isn't a true reflection of His character?

How does the truth that He is your good and perfect Father correct that misunderstanding?

DISCIPLINE, BUT NOT AS WE KNOW IT

NOW REREAD HEBREWS 12:4-11, with a focus on God's discipline. What is your initial reaction to the thought of God disciplining you?

In your own words, summarize why God's discipline of our sin is a good thing for us. (Check out Prov. 3:11-12.)

There are many reasons we find ourselves in hard places. Oftentimes they are simply the result of living in a world not yet redeemed from sin. Sometimes, though, the hard places are consequences of our own sinful choices. We live in a broken world, which means that even in Christ sin will be present and will be something we struggle with. We will miss the mark; we will fail to be Christlike. But because we are dearly loved children of a good Father, our sin no longer separates us from Him (Rom. 8). A transformation occurs when we allow the Holy Spirit to guide and convict us (2 Cor. 8). The word *discipline* in these verses means *to train, to instruct, to correct*. But why? Aren't hardships difficult enough without having to use them as case studies? Yes, they are challenging, but they are not wasted. Through trials and tribulations, we learn; we grow; we are sanctified; we are becoming more like Jesus.

When we trust God as our good, perfect, loving Father, it reframes the way we think about His discipline. And when we are able to see the pain we feel from every type of hardship as a (positive) effect of being a child of God, it empowers us to endure them in faith.

> **Nobody likes discipline or correction, but think of a way you've seen God take you through a moment of correction to refine your faith and character. What did you learn about Him? How was your relationship with Him impacted?**

Our hard places, no matter their cause, draw us to the arms of our heavenly Father. "God disciplines us for our good, in order that we may share in his holiness" (Heb. 12:10). And eventually, "it produces a harvest of righteousness and peace for those who have been trained by it" (Heb. 12:11). We are to endure hardships as discipline because in them, we are shaped into the likeness of Jesus. And so, we trust the Father with His course correction of our hearts and minds. A faith that is without wavering is built up in moments of correction that lead to wild courage.[3]

> **As you wrap up today, spend time in prayer as you consider these questions:** *How do I see God's discipline differently than I did before? Where in my life is God sharpening and strengthening my faith in Him through discipline?*

TOWARD *Holiness*

If you've spent much time in church, you're probably familiar with the term *holiness*. But like faith, this is a concept that can be hard to define. I grew up thinking holiness was a physical and behavioral definitive. Was I dressing holy enough? Was my behavior that of a "holy" person? So, when I began following Jesus, I found myself in a deep hole of shame and guilt. I sat in the church pews listening to a pastor give a sermon concerning a life of holiness, which he described as a list of behavior modifications. How would I ever live up to those expectations?

Absent from the pastor's teaching was any mention of Jesus's work on the cross as the anchor and cement that makes us holy and blameless in God's eyes. The more I studied and began to understand holiness, I realized that it didn't have anything to do with my ability to be good or do good. Rather, it has everything to do with Jesus's work on my behalf and my willingness for the Spirit to work out Christlikeness in me.

When you think about *holiness*, what are the first things that come to mind?

What do you usually associate with the pursuit of holiness?

The *Tyndale Bible Dictionary* defines *holiness* as "an inner state of freedom from moral fault and a relative harmony with the moral perfection of God."[4] In the New Testament, the term is used synonymously with *godliness*. In his book *The Pursuit of Holiness*, Jerry Bridges defines holiness as "to be morally blameless. It is to be separated from sin and, therefore, consecrated to God."[5]

Yesterday, we looked at enduring hardships as a way of being disciplined by God, instructed and course corrected. The purpose of God's correction and guidance is to transform us into the likeness of His Son, Jesus, to make us holy as He is holy (Lev. 11:44; 1 Pet. 1:16). Put another way, God's discipline is one of the ways through which we grow in holiness, and our pursuit of holiness motivates our endurance. They are all connected in our faith journey. Without holiness being fleshed out in our lives, we'd carry a hollow faith (Heb. 9:11-12; 1 John 3:2).

So, how does a faith without wavering grow through holiness?

READ HEBREWS 12:12-14 BELOW.

> Therefore, strengthen your feeble arms and weak knees. "Make level paths for your feet," so that the lame may not be disabled, but rather healed. Make every effort to live in peace with everyone and to be holy; without holiness no one will see the Lord.

In these verses, the writer of Hebrews encouraged his readers with specific ways they can strengthen their faith. What was his guidance?

OUR PURSUIT OF HOLINESS MOTIVATES OUR ENDURANCE.

NOW READ PROVERBS 4:25-27. The writer of Hebrews quoted this proverb in Hebrews 12:13. How does this passage help you better understand the guidance in Hebrews? Go back and read Hebrews 12:2 as you consider this.

Did you see it? "Fixing our eyes" (or your gaze) on Jesus! Again, we are reminded that as we grow in our relationship with God and the roots of our faith grow stronger, the key is locking our eyes on Jesus. With our eyes fixed on Him, we are able to "strengthen [our] feeble arms and weak knees" (v. 12), walk in wisdom (v. 13), "live in peace with everyone" (v. 14), and "be holy" (v. 14).

As we grow in Christlikeness, He strengthens us to weather the storms of life, to endure suffering with a courageous heart, and to grow in endurance spurred on by Him. But the question remains: What does it really look like "to be holy" (v. 14)? How do we know if we're headed in the right direction? If holiness is a key to enduring faith, it's important we know what the pursuit of holiness involves. Thankfully, Paul helps us here.

TAKE A MOMENT TO READ COLOSSIANS 3:1-17. In your own words, briefly summarize what it looks like for you to seek to live a holy and blameless life.

The key to holiness is the shift away from a life of sin and toward godliness. In Colossians 3, Paul encouraged us in this pursuit with the reminder to "set your minds on things above, not on earthly things" (v. 2). He then gave specific examples of this with the imagery of putting to death our sins and putting on characteristics of Christlikeness.

After we encounter Jesus, we are set apart to do good work as "a royal priesthood, a holy nation" (1 Pet. 2:9). His desires become our desires; His will becomes our way. Our faith is increased when we decrease (John 3:30), when we put Jesus first and seek to live a blameless life before God.

Left on our own, holiness is an exhausting, impossible endeavor. But as the Lord continues to work with us, as a potter does the clay (Isa. 64:8), we are transformed more and more into the likeness of Jesus. The result is a deep-rooted faith, one without wavering.

As you reflect on what you've learned today, prayerfully read the following verses from Psalm 66. Then, use the rest of the space on this page to write out a prayer of gratitude for the refining work God does in our lives. Ask Him to help you see His refining fire as a way He is strengthening your faith in Him.

> For You have put us to the test, God; You have refined us as silver is refined. You brought us into the net. You laid an oppressive burden upon us. You made men ride over our heads; We went through fire and through water. Yet You brought us out into a place of abundance.

PSALM 66:10-12 (NASB)

PRAYER OF GRATITUDE

(AGAIN)

"I can't get back up. I'm exhausted." The words spilled from my heart to a close friend of mine over a phone call that was long overdue. Sitting in my living room, windows slightly open, I could feel the breeze blowing through the house, the smell of the sandalwood candle along with it. I was in one of the most difficult seasons of my life, wondering if I'd ever make it to the other side. Betrayal and rejection surrounded me. Nothing made sense.

A friend and once teammate of mine knew about some of the hurt and pain caused by a former employee and yet chose to turn a blind eye to the betrayal for her own sake. A group of women I thought I was close with were subtly edging me out of their lives, and of course, there were my own family hurdles. My husband, Mario, and I were trying our best to juggle our home life and marriage while walking through season after season of difficulties with family members struggling with their mental health. All these things happening at once overwhelmed me and threw me into an identity crisis and, to be honest, a faith crisis. Worries ricocheted in my soul. My heart was tired.

> **How have you seen your faith play a role when you feel overwhelmed like this? Or how have you seen it play a role in those you look up to in the faith?**

We've seen this week how our faith is weathered by storms. I often feel like my faith is weak, hanging on like the last petal of a rose. And yet even the tiniest petal of faith is enough for God. He is the One who moves us from victims to victors. Remembering who we are in Him and the promises He has given us can sustain us through anything. I know this to be true.

Maybe you've felt this way, too. Think about the last really hard season you walked through. When you look back on it now, what word or thought comes to mind? Do you see any evidence of the Lord sustaining you and pulling you through?

We've spent most of our study so far in the book of Hebrews, but I want us to end this week by looking at the example of the apostle Paul, one of my favorite Bible friends. I admire him for his commitment and courageous faith. He is a great example for us of unwavering faith in the hard places, and we get to watch this play out in real-time in the book of Acts. Paul was one of the most influential leaders in the New Testament church, spreading the gospel far and wide, and he played a critical role in establishing the early church and wrote a large percentage of the New Testament. He devoted his life to making known the gospel of Jesus Christ to any who would listen, Jew and Gentile alike.

Acts 13 describes the beginning of Paul's missionary journey with Barnabas, an endeavor that was quickly met with hardship. The two were kicked out of Pisidian Antioch because of the uproar they'd caused with the Jews who were opposed to the gospel message (Acts 13:50). Things didn't get easier for Paul from there. Lean in because this is where we learn an important truth about faith in hardships.

READ THROUGH ACTS 14:1-20. **As you read, note one observation about Paul's ministry in Iconium (vv. 1-6) and one observation about his ministry in Lystra (vv. 7-20).**

Iconium

Lystra

In Acts 14, we find both Paul and Barnabas in Iconium, spreading the gospel of Christ Jesus, on mission for the call and the work set before them. They entered the Jewish Synagogue, as they usually did when they arrived in a new town (v. 1) but were met with opposition from both Jew and Gentile (v. 2), and after spending what Scripture describes as "considerable time" (v. 3) spreading the gospel and performing signs and wonders for the glory of God, they were forced to leave due to the unrest. Their teachings had caused division within the city, and a plot was in place to hurt both men.

Once they learned about this, they fled once again and they found themselves about a day's travel away, in Lystra. Imagine fleeing from one city, a day's travel away, only to again enter another city where you'd find even more opposition, even a threat on your life![6]

REREAD VERSE 15. What truth did the apostles proclaim about God? How do you think this truth informed their faith in Him, even under pressure?

What stands out to me in Lystra is that Paul and Barnabas could have avoided the world of hurt they endured by heeding the crowd's praise and worship of them for their healing of the man in verse 10. And yet they chose the narrow road, giving all glory back to the One who deserved it. They affirmed that God is "the living God" and the Creator of everything. And they knew their position as people sent to tell others about Him. Their faith in God drove everything.

In Acts 14:19-20 we read,

> Then some Jews came from Antioch and Iconium and won the crowd over. They stoned Paul and dragged him outside the city, thinking he was dead. *But* after the disciples had gathered around him, he got up and went back into the city. The next day he and Barnabas left for Derbe.
>
> ACTS 14:19-20 (EMPHASIS ADDED)

BUT—oh man, there's a "but."

> But after the disciples had gathered around
> him, *he got up and went back* to the city.
>
> ACTS 14:20 (EMPHASIS ADDED)

Stoned to the point of passing for dead, Paul got back up. This is unwavering faith. Back to back to back, Paul's faith was tested, tried, and trampled on by others, but that same faith is what enabled him to keep going. So, what was Paul's secret? What gave him the grit to keep on amid so much adversity? What kept him from swaying with the winds? What kept his faith intact?

I believe that Scripture shows us it was Paul's understanding of Jesus's life, death, and resurrection that made his faith resilient. Paul knew who was holding him up.

> [Jesus] was delivered over to death for our sins and
> was raised to life for our justification. Therefore,
> since we have been justified through faith, we
> have peace with God through our Lord Jesus
> Christ, through whom we have gained access by
> faith into this grace in which we now stand. And
> we boast in the hope of the glory of God.
>
> ROMANS 4:25-5:2

Paul lived his life poured out because of the grace poured out for him. Read the following words from his letter to the Romans,

> For all have sinned and fall short of the glory of
> God, and all are justified freely by his grace through
> the redemption that came by Christ Jesus. God
> presented Christ as a sacrifice of atonement, through
> the shedding of his blood—to be received *by faith*.
>
> ROMANS 3:23-25a (EMPHASIS ADDED)

This is one of Paul's beautiful summaries of the gospel. And did you catch it? There's our phrase again—*by faith*. Only here it's not talking about Old Testament faithful; it's talking about you and me! Your faith and my faith.

When you read these words, how do they inform your faith, your trust in God, and confidence in His future?

BEFORE YOU WRAP UP YOUR STUDY, READ 2 CORINTHIANS 11:24-27.
Is there a situation you feel like you're being overwhelmed by? How are you encouraged or motivated by Paul's example?

Paul went from hardship to hardship, but what carried him was his profound faith (2 Cor. 12:9-10). If we let it, hardship weathered with Christ builds up holy endurance and strength, and it makes much of Him. And in it, we begin to see that endurance is both planted and gathered because of Christ. His work and His power in and through us is the antidote for our tired soul. Today, friend, put one foot forward and let faith take you the next.

Reflection

Faith in the hard places grows and strengthens us in Christ. Remember that God can when you cannot.

1. This week we learned that God strengthens us to endure, corrects us through discipline, pushes us toward holiness, and picks us back up time and time again. Which of these feels like how God wants to work in your life today? How do you need to respond to Him?

2. What is one big takeaway or main idea you want to remember from this week of study?

3. What is one idea or thought you need to lay down that contradicts God's faithful love for you?

4. Now write out an honest prayer reflecting on the hard place you're in or a hard place you've walked through recently. Begin your prayer with praise to God for who He is, which mercifully doesn't change with your circumstances. Use the space here or a separate journal so you can look back on this prayer when you need it later.

Session Three
Video Viewer Guide
FAITH IN THE HARD PLACES

WATCH the Session Three video and take notes below.

GROUP DISCUSSION / QUESTIONS FOR REFLECTION

A leader guide is available for download at lifeway.com/withoutwavering

1. What day of personal study had the most impact on you? Why?

2. How did what you heard on the video teaching clarify, reinforce, or give new insight into what you studied this session?

3. Alexandra reminded us in this session's video teaching that "No matter the season, Christ is always King, and He is always good." How does this truth make you feel today?

4. Looking back on a recent hard place you've been in, how did you see God working in you during that time? What evidence did you see of His faithfulness and goodness? What is a lesson you learned that you need to hold onto for the next hard season?

5. Discuss your responses to the three reflection questions on page 57.

TO ACCESS THE VIDEO TEACHING SESSIONS, USE THE
INSTRUCTIONS IN THE BACK OF YOUR BIBLE STUDY BOOK.

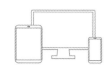

LET US RUN
WITH ENDURANCE
THE RACE THAT LIES
BEFORE US, KEEPING
OUR EYES ON JESUS,
THE PIONEER AND
PERFECTER OF
OUR FAITH.

HEBREWS 12:1-2 (CSB)

The Harvest of SPIRITUAL DISCIPLINES

Last week we considered what it looks like to have an unwavering faith in the hard seasons of life. What we didn't talk about is how God often uses our "normal" day-to-day to equip us for those more challenging seasons. That's what the rest of this study is about! While we know we're dependent on God to build up in us a faith that is without wavering, we also know from Scripture and church history that He has given us many tools that will help in this process. The spiritual disciplines are some of those tools.

The term *spiritual disciplines* is used to describe beneficial habits of the Christian life. The complete list of spiritual disciplines is long, but for this study, we're going to look at five I think are absolutely essential to strengthen our faith in the Lord and to learn to tap into His power: Bible study, prayer, worship, generosity, and service. God uses these practices to strengthen our relationship with Him and to transform us into the likeness of Jesus.[1]

SESSION 04 MEMORY VERSE

For we are God's handiwork, created in Christ Jesus to do good works, which God prepared in advance for us to do.

EPHESIANS 2:10

Bible STUDY

Many of us have a love/hate relationship with spiritual disciplines because we don't want to feel like our faith is all up to us or all about the checklists. That's why I want you to hear something important before we go any further: Spiritual disciplines aren't about forcing fruit or growth. They aren't a checklist for faith. Think of that like super gluing grapes to a grapevine; it simply doesn't work. Grapes only grow because they were birthed out of the vine. The same is true of the spiritual disciplines; they are the result of faith birthed out of relationship with Jesus and empowered by His Spirit. They are the fruit of those whose eyes are fixed on Him. Scripture is clear these practices are intentional ways God grows our faith and trust in Him. They keep us humble and remind us of our lack, and this is where we see our deep need for a Savior.

> **When you hear the term *spiritual disciplines*, which I like to think of as healthy faith habits, do you have a positive or negative gut response? Why do you think that is?**

So far in our study, we've drawn inspiration in unwavering faith from the examples of Old Testament saints, teachings from the writer of Hebrews, and from the apostle Paul. For encouragement in spiritual disciplines as a way to ground our faith in the Lord, there is no better example than the early church in Acts.

> READ ACTS 2:42-47, **the first description of the early church.**
> **List all the actions of the early church mentioned in these verses.**

In describing the early church, Luke (the writer of Acts) drew specific attention to the practices of "the apostles' teaching . . . fellowship . . . the breaking of bread . . . prayer" (v. 42), along with generosity (vv. 44-45) and service (v. 46). These practices would become foundational elements of the Christian life that continue today. Since Luke began with "the apostles' teaching," that's where we're starting too (v. 42). For us, that means Bible study. You're here, so I imagine this is a discipline you're even just a little familiar with, but it's helpful to consider why Bible study matters.

I remember the day I decided to buy my first Bible. I was eighteen years old, a new believer, zealous, eager, and curious. One day after work, I stumbled upon a Lifeway storefront at a nearby shopping center. I remember walking in and seeing home décor, gifts, and of course shelves and shelves of books and Bibles. I walked up and down the aisles exploring this new world I'd walked into. I circled the store for a while, searching for hope, truth, and direction like we all do when life seems unclear and confusing.

A few minutes went by, and I saw a woman standing over by the children's books who looked like, just maybe, she worked there. I walked up to her and was met with the kindest eyes and warmest soul. "Hi, I want to buy a Bible, but I'm not sure where to start. Can you point me in the right direction?" I asked timidly. Her face lit up with a huge smile like she'd just heard the best news. "Of course. I can help you! Follow me." She headed over to the Bibles. *There are so many of them*, I thought.

"Are you looking for a specific one?" she asked me.

"No, actually it's my first one."

She smiled again and nodded. "Today's a wonderful day for you." That lady knew exactly what I needed and reached for a leather Bible with a purple cover. She explained that it had study commentary on each page to help me understand what I was reading. I was thrilled, thanked her, paid for the Bible, and made my way home. That night I began to read the Bible, starting in John where she had suggested.

All throughout Scripture, we are commanded to be readers, students, of God's Word. Studying God's Word is such an important spiritual discipline because His Word is the way He chose to reveal Himself to us and to speak to us. With the Holy Spirit working in us, God uses the Bible to help us know Him.

LOOK UP THE FOLLOWING BIBLE PASSAGES. Next to each reference, write down what that passage has to say about the importance of studying God's Word.

PASSAGE	MAIN TAKEAWAY
Deuteronomy 11:18-21	
Joshua 1:7-8	
Psalm 1:1-3	
Romans 15:4	
2 Timothy 3:14-17	
Revelation 1:1-3	

From Moses to Revelation, the Bible is clear—what is written in God's Word must be embedded in our hearts and embodied in our lives. It is "living and effective" (Heb. 4:12, CSB), "inspired by God and . . . profitable for teaching, for rebuking, for correcting, for training in righteousness" (2 Tim. 3:16, CSB). For what purpose? "So that the man of God may be complete, equipped for every good work" (2 Tim. 3:17, CSB).

A faith without wavering is one rooted in the unshakable truth of Scripture. When firmly anchored in the Word of God, the Christian is well-positioned to navigate life and inform the world for God's glory. Like the early church's commitment to "the apostles' teaching" (Acts 2:42), God desires for us to study Scripture in the community of faithful believers (Deut. 11:18-21; Rom. 15:4). When we study His Word together, we're able to mine the profound and wonderful depths of truth that Scripture has to offer.

Here are a few of my favorite ideas for making Bible study a more regular part of your everyday. Read over them, and if one sticks out that you'd like to try this week, mark it and give it a go! You'll be so glad you did.

1. Reading Scripture is a gift. As you read this week, ask God to help you remember that you're getting to intimately know the God of all creation.

2. If you're new to studying the Bible, I suggest reading through two of my favorite Bible books, John and Hebrews.

3. When setting aside time to read and study, take bite-sized pieces of it. Read a chapter or less. As you read, remember this flow of:

OBSERVATION > INTERPRETATION > APPLICATION[2]

- What does the text say?

- What does the text mean? (This is a good place to bring in other tools, like a study Bible or Bible commentaries.)

- What does this mean for me and God's family today?

As you apply God's Word to your life, remember that God uses it to conform you to the image of Christ and equip you for every good work (Rom. 8:29; 2 Tim. 3:15-17).

4. Remember it's not a race! Take it slow and really ingest what you read.

5. Be intentional about setting aside time to read and study. Not every season will look the same for this, so give yourself grace! There is no "perfect" time to read His Word, but it is always the right time.

Prayer is always something I've wrestled with in my relationship with God, especially the question of why we're to pray. I'll never forget a day several years ago when feeling so overwhelmed by a season of life we were in that I desperately sought the Lord in prayer. That morning I walked to my car, taking deep breaths and gathering my soul for the day ahead. The leaves falling showed glimpses of a new season ahead, and as I stood outside my car door, all I could muster was a whispered, *Jesus, I know you're here, and I need you.*

That drive was a sweet moment of communion before God as I wept, wondering if change would ever come. It was a season riddled with severe anxiety, worries about one of our children who had been diagnosed with severe eye astigmatism, and seemingly constant arguments between Mario and me. I felt overlooked, undervalued, and taken for granted inside and outside of my home. Maybe you've felt this way too.

God, help me, I cried. As my heart ached for healing and hope, I communed with God in His presence. As I cried out, He leaned in to comfort me. Later that day, I asked some friends of ours to lift us up in prayer, to carry the burdens we couldn't carry. And so, they did. And we borrowed some of their faith as they reminded us of the gift our marriage is and how it is a reflection of Christ Himself.

My circumstances didn't change, but my own simple prayers and the prayers of other faithful saints helped my heart align with God and His goodness. My heart and mind were comforted, and I was able to genuinely pray, *God, Your will be done.* Sometimes, that's all we have to say, and every time, that's enough.

Moments like that one remind me why Luke emphasized prayer as a key practice of the early church throughout the book of Acts. First-century Christians faced painful, unbearable challenges as they were finding their footing in the faith, and prayer was one of the ways God united them to Him and to one another and helped them move forward.

REREAD ACTS 2:42, which we looked at yesterday. **Is prayer something you are "devoted" to? What are one or two obstacles that prevent you from having a more active prayer life?**

The phrase *they devoted themselves* has a deep sense of perseverance and steadfastness assigned to it; it was active diligence to pray with and for each other.[3] How beautiful! I can only imagine the gift it had been for the believers to gather as they saw the foundation of the church laid before them. As we read on in Acts, we get a sense of just how devoted they were to this spiritual discipline, and it's such an inspiration for us.

READ OVER THE FOLLOWING PASSAGES FROM ACTS, **highlighting each mention of prayer.**

> After they [Peter and John] were released, they went to their own people and reported everything the chief priests and the elders had said to them. When they heard this, they raised their voices together to God and said, "Master, you are the one who made the heaven, the earth, and the sea, and everything in them. . . . Lord, consider their threats, and grant that your servants may speak your word with all boldness, while you stretch out your hand for healing, and signs and wonders are performed through the name of your holy servant Jesus." When they had prayed, the place where they were assembled was shaken, and they were all filled with the Holy Spirit and began to speak the word of God boldly.
>
> ACTS 4:23-24,29-31 (CSB)

About that time King Herod violently attacked some who belonged to the church, and he executed James, John's brother, with the sword. When he saw that it pleased the Jews, he proceeded to arrest Peter too, during the Festival of Unleavened Bread. After the arrest, he put him in prison and assigned four squads of four soldiers each to guard him, intending to bring him out to the people after the Passover. So Peter was kept in prison, but the church was praying fervently to God for him. When Herod was about to bring him out for trial, that very night Peter, bound with two chains, was sleeping between two soldiers, while the sentries in front of the door guarded the prison. Suddenly an angel of the Lord appeared, and a light shone in the cell. Striking Peter on the side, he woke him up and said, "Quick, get up!" And the chains fell off his wrists.

ACTS 12:1-7 (CSB)

Now in the church at Antioch there were prophets and teachers: Barnabas, Simeon who was called Niger, Lucius of Cyrene, Manaen, a close friend of Herod the tetrarch, and Saul. As they were worshiping the Lord and fasting, the Holy Spirit said, "Set apart for me Barnabas and Saul for the work to which I have called them." Then after they had fasted, prayed, and laid hands on them, they sent them off.

ACTS 13:1-3 (CSB)

After they had preached the gospel in that town and made many disciples, they returned to Lystra, to Iconium, and to Antioch, strengthening the disciples by encouraging them to continue in the faith and by telling them, "It is necessary to go through many hardships to enter the kingdom of God." When they had appointed elders for them in every church and prayed with fasting, they committed them to the Lord in whom they had believed.

ACTS 14:21-23 (CSB)

About midnight Paul and Silas were praying and singing hymns to God, and the prisoners were listening to them. Suddenly there was such a violent earthquake that the foundations of the jail were shaken, and immediately all the doors were opened, and everyone's chains came loose. When the jailer woke up and saw the doors of the prison standing open, he drew his sword and was going to kill himself, since he thought the prisoners had escaped. But Paul called out in a loud voice, "Don't harm yourself, because we're all here!" The jailer called for lights, rushed in, and fell down trembling before Paul and Silas. He escorted them out and said, "Sirs, what must I do to be saved?"

ACTS 16:25-30 (CSB)

Looking over these verses, how would you summarize the purpose of prayer as modeled by the early church? (Don't try to come up with "the right answer" here; just write down what you observe.)

At its most simple explanation, prayer is the way God's children talk to Him. In these verses, we see the early church praising God through prayer, voicing bold prayers for God to act, praying for gospel ministry to go forth, and praying as part of their worship together. Prayer strengthens our faith by firmly rooting us in the One from whom our strength comes. It's an act of surrender, admitting to God that we can't but He can. Prayer is worship and thanksgiving, giving glory to the uncreated Creator. Prayer is the lifeline to our souls—in it, we participate with God in His power, and the prayer is moved by His presence.

When we pray, we're reminding our hearts and minds that we have a need that can only be filled by and in Jesus. It's a spiritual discipline that reminds us we are needy creatures dependent on our Creator. I can't help but wonder if our generation of believers undervalues the gift found in the life and faith of a devoted prayer. Do we miss it in our hurry to keep up with the world around us? Is it central to what we do when we gather together? Is it the primary way we encourage and support others? Or do we believe that maybe our performance and hustle will outdo God's will and power? Do we wonder if He's even really listening?

In Philippians 4:6-7 (CSB), Paul wrote,

> Don't worry about anything, but in everything, through prayer and petition with thanksgiving, present your requests to God. And the peace of God, which surpasses all understanding, will guard your hearts and minds in Christ Jesus.

What does this verse tell us about prayer? About God's desire and purpose for us in it?

What are some specific ways prayer strengthens your faith?

AS WE PRAY, WE FIX OUR GAZE ON JESUS, AND WE ROOT OURSELVES MORE DEEPLY IN HIM.

Prayer *does* matter, and God *is* listening. As we pray, we fix our gaze on Jesus, and we root ourselves more deeply in Him. If prayer is a habit we develop now, then when the storms of life come, when our faith is tested and tried, our natural response will be to worship God through prayer. As you go about your day, think about God, invite Him into your day, and talk to Him. Thank Him for what was, and is, and is to come in Him.

A common hurdle to prayer is worrying that you don't know the "right" words to say to God. But the great news is that it doesn't matter! He really just wants you to talk to Him. And the more you explore prayer in Scripture, some helpful patterns become evident. I love the **ACTS model for prayer:** Adoration, Confession, Thanksgiving, Supplication.

Spend a few minutes talking with God now, using this pattern as a guide.

A	ADORATION	Praise God for who He is and how He works.
C	CONFESSION	Confess any recent sins to God, and accept the forgiveness He's extending to you.
T	THANKSGIVING	Thank God for the redemption from sins that is yours because of Jesus. Then talk to Him about things you're thankful for today.
S	SUPPLICATION	Ask God to work out His will in given situations and to help align you and others with whatever His will may be.

Worship

When most of us think about *worship*, this word holds many of our Sunday morning core memories—gathering together to sing songs of praise to God as a way to lift up our thanksgiving and weariness and remind ourselves of the hope we have in Christ Jesus. And yes, that's a huge part of what it means to worship God. However, singing songs and gathering together just scrapes the surface of what worship involves.

Missing the heart behind worship is a big obstacle to living a life of abiding in Christ. Here's what I mean: Consider the events of that year we'll never forget—2020. We faced the onslaught of a global pandemic, a divisive political climate, and conflicting views on social injustices. Heated opinions flooded our churches, dinner tables, and especially our social media. The world—and worse, the church—turned in on itself.

As Christians, we were faced with a challenge: *How do we lovingly and worshipfully move through nuances and tensions while keeping Christ at the center of our actions?* We found ourselves angry and confused. The church felt the tension around us, and many of us had to consider if we were willing to stay on the way of love (the harder road, am I right?) and continue to bear witness to the love of Christ through truth *and* grace. Or would we allow our pride and opinions to deter us from walking the narrow road? Only when our hearts are rightly oriented in worship before the Lord are we able to consistently choose the hard road of love.

READ OVER ACTS 2:42-47, where we've been focused this week. In what ways do we see the early church worshiping God here? How was their worship reflective of their love for God?

Mario and I have had many conversations about the concept of living all of life as worship. When our son was about ten months old, we began to attend a church that embodied what Acts 2:42-47 talks about. The emphasis wasn't just worshiping on Sundays; it was an invitation to live all of life as worship in fellowship with one another.

The first-century Christians help us see how our study of the Word, our fellowship, our hospitality, and our generosity are ways we worship God, ways we praise and prioritize Him.

> LOOK UP AND READ ACTS 16:16-34. **List all the different ways you see Paul and Silas worshiping God in this scene. What stands out to you? Does anything surprise you?**

This snapshot from Paul's ministry is a great example for us of living a life of worship. The message of the gospel was spreading and the church was growing, and yet (or because of this) Paul and the other apostles faced opposition as they shared the good news and worked miracles in Jesus's name. Paul and Silas worshiped God in all they did—as they met needs, in their teaching and service, and even from jail. Everything they did was out of love and devotion to God.

Living a life of worship is living a life surrendered to the will of God. It makes much of Jesus, honoring His precious and perfect work. Perhaps we've lost sight of this posture? Maybe worship has become more of a Sunday morning performance than the practice to live a life of honor to God? Let's flesh this out some.

> READ THE PASSAGES OF SCRIPTURE ON THE FOLLOWING PAGE. **Next to each one, note what it teaches you about worship.**

SCRIPTURE	What did you learn about worship?
Ascribe to the LORD the glory due his name; bring an offering and come before him. Worship the LORD in the splendor of his holiness. **1 CHRONICLES 16:29 (NIV)**	
Come, let's shout joyfully to the LORD, shout triumphantly to the rock of our salvation! Let's enter his presence with thanksgiving; let's shout triumphantly to him in song. For the LORD is a great God, a great King above all gods. The depths of the earth are in his hand, and the mountain peaks are his. The sea is his; he made it. His hands formed the dry land. Come, let's worship and bow down; let's kneel before the LORD our Maker. **PSALM 95:1-6 (CSB)**	
Therefore, brothers and sisters, in view of the mercies of God, I urge you to present your bodies as a living sacrifice, holy and pleasing to God; this is your true worship. Do not be conformed to this age, but be transformed by the renewing of your mind, so that you may discern what is the good, pleasing, and perfect will of God. **ROMANS 12:1-2 (CSB)**	
Above all, put on love, which is the perfect bond of unity. And let the peace of Christ, to which you were also called in one body, rule your hearts. And be thankful. Let the word of Christ dwell richly among you, in all wisdom teaching and admonishing one another through psalms, hymns, and spiritual songs, singing to God with gratitude in your hearts. And whatever you do, in word or in deed, do everything in the name of the Lord Jesus, giving thanks to God the Father through him. **COLOSSIANS 3:14-17 (CSB)**	
I heard every creature in heaven, on earth, under the earth, on the sea, and everything in them say, Blessing and honor and glory and power be to the one seated on the throne, and to the Lamb, forever and ever! The four living creatures said, "Amen," and the elders fell down and worshiped. **REVELATION 5:13-14 (CSB)**	

A life of worship is a life surrendered to Christ in every form and fashion. Just like Paul and Silas in Acts 16, worship often happens in moments we least expect it—moments when we choose to offer forgiveness, testify to God's goodness, or offer up thanksgiving to God no matter our situation or circumstance. It's not an act; it's a lifestyle and attribute of someone who follows Jesus.

As you wrap up your study today, ask yourself the following questions. Sit with them and prayerfully reflect on what needs to change for you to live your life as more of an act of worship to the Lord.

1. How can I live a life of worship through my actions and words?

2. What do I need to surrender today in order to make room to love God and love His people well?

Generosity & SERVICE

Today we're considering two more spiritual disciplines, habits that help us grow in Christlikeness, live in faithful obedience, and support the body of Christ—*generosity* and *service*. Like all the disciplines we've looked at this week, these two are modeled on the example of Jesus, who:

> . . . emptied himself by assuming the form of
> a servant, taking on the likeness of humanity. And
> when he had come as a man, he humbled himself
> by becoming obedient to the point of death . . .
>
> PHILIPPIANS 2:7-8 (CSB)

Jesus lived a life of generosity and service, and He calls His church to do the same by faith and through grace.

GENEROSITY—GIVING AWAY WHAT YOU'VE BEEN GIVEN

My youngest, Sophia, is one of the most giving children. She lends a hand when it's needed and often when it's not. Unwarranted, you'll find our youngest girl giving her words and service at the most perfect times. She's typically overzealous in her giving; it flows. But there are also moments in which she defaults to the natural bent toward selfishness we all have—moments that take me back because I don't see them coming from her, moments when giving is too much of a sacrifice, when it comes between her and something she loves or desires.

We expect this from a child, but many of us grown-ups—myself included—respond this way when we're asked to give. We're willing to give of our time, talent, and treasure when it's convenient or when we have excess; that's simple enough. But at the minimal sign of inconvenience or sacrifice, we shrink back, allowing things like fear of lack or fear of being taken advantage of or undervalued to take

JESUS LIVED A LIFE OF GENEROSITY AND SERVICE, AND HE CALLS HIS CHURCH TO DO THE SAME.

over. We protect ourselves and our possessions—both physical and emotional. That's when we see our true posture in living generously.

So, what is God's desire for us when it comes to generosity? And how does that posture increase our faith in Him?

READ ACTS 2:44-45 AND ACTS 4:32-35. What stands out to you in these two passages? What clues do you see as to the early church's motivation for generosity?

As the church began to grow and spread, generosity was at the heart of their community. The believers were "one in heart and mind" (4:32), not claiming anything they had as their own and sharing everything they had (2:44-45). Times were tough, and yet togetherness, building the church, was not just a priority but a way of life.

Acts 4:33 says they were continuously hearing the apostles testify about the good news. Generosity was one of the ways they responded to the gospel; it was a response of thanksgiving and gratefulness because the greatest cost had been paid. They freely gave because they already had everything they needed. They gave of their time and talent and treasure. It was all God's anyway.

NOW READ ACTS 4:36–5:11. Write down a few thoughts as you compare Barnabas (4:36-37) with Ananias and Sapphira (5:1-11).

When you examine your heart, does it look more like Barnabas's or Ananias's?

To help us understand that generosity is a matter of the heart, Luke compared the humble, generous spirit of Barnabas with the selfish, deceptive spirit of Ananias and Sapphira. Giving is an act of faith—we give as a part of God's communal family, seeing the needs of others as an opportunity to bear witness to the work of Christ, and we trust that as we give God will continue to take care of us.

When we give, we're exercising our faith muscle by living from a posture of thanksgiving because of how much God has given us. God calls us to give of our time, talents, and treasures to support the ministry of the gospel while we wait for Jesus to come back (Matt. 25:14-30). With our eyes fixed on Jesus, we give open-handedly, believing in the God who gives us everything we need.

SERVICE—PUTTING OTHERS FIRST

NOW READ ACTS 5:12–6:7. **While you read, look for examples of service in the early church.**

The spiritual disciplines of generosity and service go hand in hand because both are about using what God has given you to take care of others. A life of serving is a life of worship. It embodies showing up in ways that one would think are small and inconspicuous. These ways aren't always at service events at your church or in your community. Sometimes, serving looks like helping a neighbor out who needs an extra hand. Sometimes, it's being the hands and feet of a mom who is overwhelmed and needs some extra support. Other times, it's the minutes and hours we sacrifice to lean in, regardless of the ask or the task.

A LIFE OF SERVING IS A LIFE OF WORSHIP.

READ PHILIPPIANS 2:1-11. **As in everything, Jesus is our ultimate example of a servant heart. What do you learn from His example?**

When we offer our lives up to serving, we move past the physical and enter in the work of Christ in the heavenly realms. How? By bearing witness to heaven on earth, pushing back the darkness with the evidence of Christ's servant-hearted love for us all. As you serve and show up as the hands and feet of Christ, you are the answer to someone's prayer.

Examine your heart. What is the biggest obstacle—a sin, a fear, an attitude—that makes a lifestyle of service challenging for you?

As we end this session, think about the example of the early church in Acts 4 and 5. Come up with at least one answer to each of the questions below. Then, share your responses with someone in your Bible study group, your church community, or your family so you have accountability.

What is God calling you to give this week? What does He want you to sacrifice for the advancement of the gospel and/or the good of the church?

Where is God calling you to serve this week? Who needs to see the love of Jesus through your intentionality and a helping hand?

FURTHER STUDY

In our study this week, we considered five spiritual disciplines that have been a part of Christian life since the earliest days of the faith—Bible study, prayer, worship, giving, and serving. But these aren't the only disciplines worth practicing!

While it's hard to pen a complete list, here are some of the others that empower you to "grow in the grace and knowledge of our Lord and Savior Jesus Christ" (2 Pet. 3:18):

- **CONFESSION:** Confession of sin, both to God and to others in Christian fellowship.

- **FASTING:** Laying aside of food for a period of time in order to seek to know God in a deeper experience.[4]

- **FELLOWSHIP:** "The bond of common purpose and devotion that binds Christians together and to Christ."[5]

- **REMEMBRANCE:** Setting aside time "to dwell on who God has always been and what He has done."[6]

- **SCRIPTURE MEMORIZATION:** Memorizing Bible verses so God's Word is always in your head and on your heart.

- **SOLITUDE:** "To consciously pull away from everything else in our lives . . . for the purpose of giving our full and undivided attention to God.[7]

- **SIMPLICITY:** Freeing us to live our days fully devoted to the Lord, so nothing prevents us from investing in what's eternal.[8]

As you grow in faith and incorporate these and other disciplines into your relationship with the Lord, remember,

> The focus is not on undertaking them correctly or attempting to impress God or others but rather on seeking to practice them with gratitude. Jesus demonstrates the importance of spiritual disciplines in his own life by cultivating his relationship with God through various practices, including prayer, meditation on and memorization of Scripture, discernment, solitude and retreat, service, celebration, and public worship. . . . Disciplines can become holy habits that train people to grow.[9]

TOM SCHWANDA

Reflection

Spiritual disciplines keep us humble and remind us of our lack, and this is where we see our deep need for a Savior. They aren't about forcing fruit or growth. They aren't a checklist for faith. They are the result of faith birthed out of relationship with Jesus and empowered by His Spirit. They are the fruit of those whose eyes are fixed on Him.

1. Flip back through your week of study and reflect on each day's closing activity. Where are you now in your habits, and what growth would you like to see? In what areas and/or habits do you feel the Lord leading you to be sharpened? Who is someone you can partner with for accountability?

2. What is one big takeaway or main idea you want to remember from this week of study?

3. What is one idea or thought you need to lay down that contradicts God's faithful love for you?

4. Now use your remaining time to practice the ACTS model for prayer: Adoration, Confession, Thanksgiving, Supplication. Focus your supplication prayers on your desire to grow in your faith and in your practice of spiritual disciplines.

WATCH the Session Four video and take notes below.

GROUP DISCUSSION / QUESTIONS FOR REFLECTION

A leader guide is available for download at lifeway.com/withoutwavering

1. What day of personal study had the most impact on you? Why?

2. How did what you heard on the video teaching clarify, reinforce, or give new insight into what you studied this session?

3. Of the spiritual disciplines we considered this week—Bible study, prayer, worship, giving, and serving—which one do you sense the Spirit encouraging you to prioritize? What is one way you plan to do that this week?

4. In the video, Alexandra pointed out, "Spiritual rhythms aren't about doing for God, but about being with God. They are spiritual deposits made into the banks of our souls." What keeps you from investing in spiritual disciplines? How can we encourage each other to make time for this good work?

5. Discuss your responses to the three reflection questions on page 84.

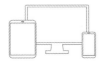

TO ACCESS THE VIDEO TEACHING SESSIONS, USE THE
INSTRUCTIONS IN THE BACK OF YOUR BIBLE STUDY BOOK.

Building Resilience through
FAITHFUL OBEDIENCE

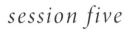

This week, we will consider a life of faithful obedience to the Lord. What does it look like to say yes to God over the long haul? To let trust in Him guide our every step? Taking some cues from the examples of Abraham and Sarah, we'll see that the more we walk with God and familiarize ourselves with His promises, the more we trust that God is in it and up to something—that He not only sees us but also cares for us.

Unwavering faith is about trust—trust in the character of God, His promises, and His faithfulness to those promises. To faithfully follow Jesus is to live a life marked by long-suffering love and holy perseverance. This unwavering faith we long for is found in the surrender that comes with daily obedience to Him.

SESSION 05 MEMORY VERSE

I am the vine; you are the branches. If you remain in me and I in you, you will bear much fruit; apart from me you can do nothing.

JOHN 15:5

THE CALL TO *Faith*

Recently I was speaking at a church conference where I closed the message by commissioning listeners to reflect on how a life on mission for Christ is a life of surrender. As the words left my mouth, I knew this word was also very much for me. I'd been praying and asking God for direction, for a clear next step, related to some challenging relationships in my life. Was it time to sever the relationships? To give them to God? I'd tried for so long to salvage them, to lean in, to help them. I'd felt like God was asking me to listen, to wait, to trust. As I struggled to wait, I had a deep sense of discontentment. The control I thought I had over those relationships was slipping through my hands.

God was calling me to trust Him, but trust without seeing doesn't come easily for me. The phrase "blind faith" is one I'm quick to push back against. I don't believe God wants blind faith from us, because I believe He calls us to look back—to remember His works and His word. To see the pictures of His faithfulness in Scripture and in our own lives. This is what He was asking of me then, and He continues to ask it of me now. To believe Him, to take Him at His word. Moments when we're reminded that we don't have control are the moments God uses to remind us of His faithfulness and to water and tend to our faith. This is how it grows into a faith unshakable—resilient, confident, and obedient.

The assurance of our faith ought to come naturally when we consider examples from the Bible like Abraham, but it often doesn't. He was given promises by God, and history proved those oaths to be true. Over the next few days, we'll watch as Abraham was called to step out in faith time and again and responded in obedience. Let's begin with the first time God called him to obey.

READ GENESIS 12:1-5. **What did God instruct Abram (God changed his name to Abraham later) to do, and how did Abram respond? Note any words that stand out to you in these verses.**

What assumptions can we make about Abram's relationship with God based on his obedience to God's calling?

"So Abram went" (v. 4). This verse has always stood out to me. When I look at Abram's relationship with God, I see a deep resolve from Abram to trust God no matter what. Bible commentator Matthew Henry, reflecting on Genesis 12:4, wrote, "His obedience was speedy and without delay, submissive and without dispute; for he *went out, not knowing whither he went* (Heb. 11:8), but knowing whom he followed and under whose direction he went."[1]

NOW READ HEBREWS 11:8-10, PRINTED HERE.

> By faith Abraham, when he was called, obeyed and set out for a place that he was going to receive as an inheritance. He went out, even though he did not know where he was going. By faith he stayed as a foreigner in the land of promise, living in tents as did Isaac and Jacob, coheirs of the same promise. For he was looking forward to the city that has foundations, whose architect and builder is God (CSB).

What insight did the writer of Hebrews add to Genesis 12? How do you think the promise God made (Gen. 12:1-3) helped establish Abraham's faith and fueled his obedient response?

Hebrews 11:8-10 teaches us that like Abraham, our surrender to God—our trust or faith in Him—precedes our obedience. We may not always know what's next, or where we're going, but God does, and He can be trusted. Abraham believed God and clung to the promises that God would give him the land and make him into a great nation. His confidence in God's faithfulness motivated his own faith. In the book of Romans, Paul helped connect some of these dots for us.

READ ROMANS 4. Summarize what Paul said about Abraham's example of faith. (Look closely at verses 3,5,18,20-21.)

In Romans 4, Paul used the example of Abraham to show readers how faith and trust in God have always been the key marker of relationship with Him. John Piper explains, "When Paul said in Romans 4:20 that Abraham was strengthened (passive voice) in his faith, giving glory to God, that passive voice is intended to draw our attention to the fact that this amazing work of faith in Abraham was not just his doing; it was the work of God in him. . . . Paul is showing us that this faith itself is a work of God, so that in the end God gets all the glory."[2]

What can you take from Abraham's example in Genesis 12 and Paul's teaching in Romans 4 and apply to your own relationship with the Lord?

The emphasis in Genesis 12 and throughout Abraham's story is not on the amount of faith Abraham had, but on whom he placed his faith. He believed wholeheartedly that "God had power to do what he had promised" (Rom. 4:21). Because his faith was rooted in the one true God, "he did not waver through unbelief" (4:20). Abraham trusted God enough to believe the promise that all the nations of the earth would be blessed in him, even though he had no offspring when that promise was made. And as time went by and an heir remained absent, Abraham still faithfully trusted God to fulfill the promises made to him, even though it seemed increasingly impossible.

In Hebrews 6:15, we are told, "And so, after waiting patiently, Abraham obtained the promise" (CSB). Abraham had to be patient with God to allow Him time and room to do His work. Abraham had to trust God to be who He says He is. That's exactly what Abraham did, and why he is the ultimate example of faithful obedience for us.

What can you learn from Abraham when your patience for God's timing begins to wear thin, when you're struggling to wait on God's promises?

We're all called to a daily assignment, first and foremost, to love God and His people (Matt. 22:36-40; Matt. 28:16-20). Doing that is how we obey in the small moments of our lives. Then, there are other times when obedience is harder, when nothing makes sense, but God is calling you to put one foot in front of the other and to simply trust Him. Faithful obedience to God is found in our yes to Him in those small everyday steps and the big leaps of faith He asks us to take.

Today, take time to recall who God is and who you are in Him. What motivates your steps of obedience?

In what ways might God be asking you to trust Him today and live out obedience? Is today a small everyday step or a big leap of faith?

FAITH IN

God's Promises

I often joke that I have the gift of unbelief. I'm kidding; it's not a gift, but it is a struggle! A few years ago, I found myself arguing with my husband in our kitchen. The sun was setting, and what I remember most was the gold that I saw coming through the back windows of the house. I was in a season where life had little to no direction. I had spent most of my young adult years planning for what was to come, but like most of us, plans hadn't gone, well, as planned. I was confused about the direction my life was going in, or lack thereof. I was young, zealous, and wanted nothing more than to take the right next step. And I was taking out my frustration on Mario.

In today's study, we look to our friend Sarah, Abraham's wife. The picture we get of her in Genesis leads us to believe her faith wavered more than her husband's, which makes her very relatable in my opinion. Looking back at her life, I see so much of my need to control, to create a good probable outcome, to work out my faith on my own. Her lack of trust looks a lot like mine. And yet! Sarah's faith was commendable enough to be highlighted for us in God's Word. What encouragement.

LOOK UP AND READ THE FOLLOWING PASSAGES OF SCRIPTURE
and think through the questions that follow.

GENESIS 11:30 | GENESIS 15:3-6 | GENESIS 16:1-4

What was the primary obstacle Sarah (then Sarai) faced to faithful obedience?

How did Sarah see herself fitting into God's promise to Abraham (then Abram)?

In Genesis 11, we learn that Sarai (whom God later renamed Sarah in Gen. 17:15) was barren, something considered a devastating curse in their culture.[3] The promise God made her husband was about making him into a great nation (Gen. 12:1-3; 15:1-6), so I imagine it was hard for her to see what possible role she could play in the fulfillment of that promise. The result? Sarai took matters into her own hands (Gen. 16). She approached her servant Hagar in what seems like an effort to bring forth the promise through her. Sarai gave Hagar to Abram as a wife. Maybe Abram and Sarai thought that this "plan B" could be what got them to the promise—*perhaps taking Hagar as a wife was a logical plan, or even part of God's plan all along?*[4]

Even though Abram and Sarai had faith in God, they still went to great lengths to assist God in bringing His promise to fulfillment. I know what you're thinking: *I would never go out of my way to try and manipulate a situation in God's plan!* But we do, don't we? The actions are different, but the posture and intent are the same. Like Sarai, we struggle to believe God is true to His word, and we often act like we are better at being God than God. But God didn't need Sarai's help to fulfill His promise, and He doesn't need ours. He invites us to play a role in His perfect plan, but it's not perfect if we're the ones doing the planning.

> **How does Sarai's story impact the way you see the working out of your own faith? Do you resonate with her need for control or her manipulation of circumstances? What do those types of feelings reveal about your trust in God?**

> **What is an instance when you can see yourself offering God a plan B or maybe even executing it?**

I am the queen of plan Bs and contingency plans. I don't remember a time when I've totally trusted God with my whole life. I've offered up course-corrections when all the while God was course-correcting me. I can relate to Sarah's story so much—more than I'd like—striving my way to God's perfect will while He's the Giver of it. When I begin to feel out of control and really afraid of what's to come, I go back to Matthew 6:28-33 and remember Jesus's encouraging words:

> And why do you worry about clothes? Observe how the wildflowers of the field grow: They don't labor or spin thread. Yet I tell you that not even Solomon in all his splendor was adorned like one of these. If that's how God clothes the grass of the field, which is here today and thrown into the furnace tomorrow, won't he do much more for you—you of little faith? So don't worry, saying, "What will we eat?" or "What will we drink?" or "What will we wear?" For the Gentiles eagerly seek all these things, and your heavenly Father knows that you need them. But seek first the kingdom of God and his righteousness, and all these things will be provided for you. (CSB).

Our heavenly Father cares for us, for every detail of our lives. When we can't see the way ahead or wrestle with doubts of God's faithfulness or the goodness of His plan, we must remind ourselves that we can trust in God's promises, for He is faithful.

NOW READ HEBREWS 11:11:

> And by faith even Sarah, who was past childbearing age, was enabled to bear children because she considered him faithful who had made the promise.

According to the writer of Hebrews, what was Sarah's faith rooted in?

GOD INVITES US TO PLAY A ROLE IN HIS PERFECT PLAN, BUT IT'S NOT PERFECT IF WE'RE THE ONES DOING THE PLANNING.

Sarah's faithful waiting hinged on the faithful character of God (Heb. 11:11). Although she had no way to know when God would act or the role she would play, even in her doubt, the text tells us she believed in God's faithfulness.

Like Abraham and Sarah, we also have a faith rooted in promises. Some that have been fulfilled—like all of the Old Testament promises that point forward to Jesus, the Savior—but some that remain unfulfilled. My hope is that we can learn to be people like Abraham and Sarah, people whose faith is rooted in the Promise Maker. People whose faith is strengthened not in outcomes, but in the process of becoming more like Christ, and playing a role in God's plan to fulfill His great promise to us—a family of every nation, tribe, and tongue worshiping Him forever (Rev. 5:9). We are not promised a life without problems, but we are promised God is walking with us through it all.

Prayerfully reflect on the following words from Paul, words of hope that can fuel your faith through even the hardest days.

For our light and momentary troubles are achieving for us an eternal glory that far outweighs them all. So we fix our eyes not on what is seen, but on what is unseen, since what is seen is temporary, but what is unseen is eternal.

2 CORINTHIANS 4:17-18

FURTHER STUDY

The promises of God form the backbone of our faith. From the opening chapters of Genesis to the close of Revelation, the Bible is full of promises from God. While too many to list here, this chart includes a few that simply can't be missed. I encourage you to read through the Scripture passages listed here at your own pace between now and the time you finish this Bible study. If you're unsure of God's promise in any passage, use a study Bible or look up the passage online.[5]

PASSAGE	PROMISE
GENESIS 3:15	
GENESIS 12:1-7	
2 SAMUEL 7	
JEREMIAH 31:31-37	
JOHN 14:1-3	
2 PETER 3:1-13	
REVELATION 21:3-5	

THE SACRIFICE
of Faith

I don't like to talk about sacrifice, and I especially don't like having to walk it out. Giving up our interests, our time, our will, and possibly even our lives for others is one of the most uncomfortable realities we face in the Christian life. From early childhood, it's evident the idea of sacrifice is a struggle. Why do I have to share? Why do we have to put others first? Why should we listen to someone else? Why is my yes less important than your no? Why must we stop doing what we want to do in order to be obedient to what we must do?

As recently as the day before I wrote these words, I found myself in negotiations with God because I know He's asking for sacrifice from me. I've wrestled with my current season of life for what seems like almost a decade. A lack of clarity and direction in ministry, with a side of uncomfortable circumstances, has worn down my heart. Things haven't been going as planned; friendships are falling apart; family is hard. I wanted out of the discomfort, out of the lack of clarity, out of the tunnel that only offered a dim light at the end. As I talked to the Lord about this, I sensed Him asking, *Are you willing to consider My desires? Are you willing to sacrifice your fear and need for control in order to trust Me?*

When God asks us to trust Him, He challenges us to sacrifice our need to be in control in a holy exchange for a deeper faith.

> **Think about a recent sacrifice you've had to make (or maybe should have made but resisted). What were some of the feelings you wrestled with through that experience?**

In Genesis 21–22, we read a story that helps us feel the tension of surrender and trust. Our friends Abraham and Sarah clung to the promise that God would give them an heir, the first step in building God's "great nation" (Gen. 12:2). Although they attempted to do it their own way, resulting in the birth of Ishmael to Sarah's servant Hagar (Gen. 16), God remained faithful to His promise, and Sarah eventually gave birth to their son, Isaac (Gen. 21:1-3).

> Now the LORD was gracious to Sarah as he had said,
> and the LORD did for Sarah what he had promised.
>
> GENESIS 21:1

This short verse beautifully sums up the faithfulness of God. He "did for Sarah what he had promised." He was faithful to Abraham and Sarah, and He is faithful to you and me.

NOW READ GENESIS 22:1-4. **Can you imagine? Write down a few words that capture how Abraham might have felt in this moment as he processed God's instructions.**

READ VERSE 1 AGAIN. **What word reveals the reason God told Abraham to sacrifice Isaac?**

In a test of his faith, God told Abraham to do the unimaginable. God instructed him to sacrifice his long-awaited and prayed-for son, Isaac—the child of promise born into Abraham's family. I imagine fear, confusion, and even anger being emotions Abraham felt at that moment, but we don't know. What we do know is that Abraham's trust didn't seem to waver, and "early the next morning" he stepped out in faithful obedience and walked the road of sacrifice. What we see next is incredible.

READ GENESIS 22:5-18. **List a couple of observations you have about Abraham from this story.**

REREAD VERSES 12 AND 16-18. Summarize God's response to Abraham's obedience in your own words.

I believe that Abraham's willing disposition was only because of His profound trust in the Lord. He'd seen God move—he knew God's heart—and so he gave his all, knowing that God would do the same. "When they reached the mountain, Abraham told his servant, 'Stay here with the donkey; I and the boy will go over there and worship and come again to you' (Gen. 22:5). Notice how the text includes both Abraham and 'the boy,' Isaac, in the return journey."[6]

The *ESV Study Bible* notes of this verse, "While Abraham is committed to sacrificing Isaac, he plans to do so in the belief that both of them will return."[7] Abraham had seen God move before—he saw God's faithfulness through the provision of a new homeland and the birth of Isaac. He had no reason to believe this time would be any different, but I can't even begin to imagine how hard these steps of faith would have been. We see in Abraham a confidence in God that empowered him to say, "We will come back." His faith was built up over years of obedience, which gave him the confidence to step into the next storm.

READ HEBREWS 11:17-19. What does this passage tell you that Abraham believed about the character of God?

How does Abraham's faith and testimony in Genesis 22 equip you to walk in obedience?

Abraham had experienced God in his detours, doubts, and delays (Gen. 17:17; 21:5). His faith was not blind. In fact, it was clear and anchored. For us, God's future promise to make all things right is where we drop our anchor; it's the truth we hold onto. And we know God will be faithful to this promise because of the work Jesus already accomplished through His death and resurrection.

> So also Christ, having been offered once to bear the sins of many, will appear a second time, not to bear sin, but to bring salvation to those who are waiting for him.
>
> HEBREWS 9:28 (CSB)

God's desire when asking us to sacrifice and surrender isn't to take from us but to add to our relationship with Him. See, in God's economy, subtraction isn't about taking away; rather it's about making room for the addition, for God's will and best to flesh out. And every time, regardless of the external outcome, if postured with a willing heart, we're left with a more robust and deep faith.

What is a situation or challenge in your life that God may be asking you to release control of in order to trust Him? How can you practically trust God to move in that space? For example, what can you do to get out of God's way?

God reveals Himself to us as we follow Him. When we can't see the next step, God does, and so we simply follow Him, love Him, and love His people. Don't let fear in the unknown keep you from living life free in obedience and surrender. God is faithful—He always has been, and He always will be. So today, instead of worrying or trying to manipulate a situation, pray, and surrender it to God.

THE PROMISE
of Faith

You know what's powerful? Proof. Mile markers and evidence. When we're doubting or wondering if something is true, proof is what we go looking for.

In one of my counseling sessions a few years back, my therapist asked, "What will it take for you to see grace in your story?" I sat there, wondering how to even conceptualize the question. We'd been talking through the depths of my journey, my layers of unbelief coupled with the bitterness that had taken root in my heart. What does *grace* mean, and where was it? Healing from past wounds is difficult. Wounds from your family are always the hardest to heal from, and then you tag on a few fresh wounds from church, and, man, it can be hard to see. I think part of the problem is that it can be hard for us to understand.

> **Give your best effort at a definition of GRACE. Without looking it up in a dictionary or googling it, write down a statement that describes the grace of God.**

Grace, like *faith*, is one of those spiritual terms you hear thrown around a lot in Christian circles but can be hard to put into words, isn't it? Here's a helpful explanation:

> Grace has to do with God's divine response to the
> world that enables Him to confront sin with a limitless
> capacity to forgive and bless, which He has done through
> the sacrificial death and resurrection of Jesus.[8]

And here's a Bible dictionary definition that I find helpful:

> Grace is "undeserved acceptance and love received from
> another, especially the characteristic attitude of God
> in providing salvation for sinners. For Christians, the
> word "grace" is virtually synonymous with the gospel of
> God's gift of unmerited salvation in Jesus Christ."[9]

Because of God's grace in my life, I'm able to look back at my story through the lens of God's bigger story. My counselor was asking me to take note of Jesus's presence and power: He'd always been there, loving me through. Even in moments of pain and disillusion, God's grace is what carries us. Grace feels far when pain is so present, but I can attest that it's always there, not just as a cushion to catch you but as a balm to restore you. It mends and binds up the scars that life leaves on you. The story of Scripture shows us how, from the very beginning of time, God's fingerprints of grace have been on the world bringing every promise to fulfillment.

READ GENESIS 12:1-3, **printed below. Remember, this is the initial promise God made to Abraham, which we studied earlier in the week.**

The Lord had said to Abram, "Go from your country,
your people and your father's household to the land
I will show you. "I will make you into a great nation,
and I will bless you; I will make your name great,
and you will be a blessing. I will bless those who
bless you, and whoever curses you I will curse; and
all peoples on earth will be blessed through you."

What evidence of God's grace do you see in this promise He made to Abraham? Underline any phrases that make you think about Jesus.

Like so many moments in the Old Testament, God's promise in Genesis 12 points forward to God's redemptive work through Jesus the Messiah. This is a continuation of another promise He made all the way back in the garden of Eden.

> And I will put enmity between you and the woman,
> and between your offspring and hers; he will crush
> your head, and you will strike his heel.

GENESIS 3:15

These were God's words to the serpent after he lured Adam and Eve into sin. God promised a seed, or an offspring, who would defeat the serpent, Satan, and reverse the curse of sin and death. The promise to bless "all peoples on earth" through Abraham was the next step in God's plan for redemption through the promised offspring. We get yet another glimpse of this redemption thread later in Abraham's story.

REREAD GENESIS 22:7-14 **from yesterday's study. Where do you see God hinting at Jesus in this scene?**

As I read Genesis 22:7, I can't help but think about God's sacrifice for us through the Lamb, His Son Jesus. With parallel language, the Gospel of John draws a striking connection between God's test of Abraham and God's fulfillment of the promise: "The next day John saw Jesus coming toward him and said, 'Look, the Lamb of God, who takes away the sin of the world!'" (John 1:29). God provided the sacrifice so that Isaac wouldn't have to die. Generations later, He again provided a Lamb, that time so we wouldn't have to be the ones to die (John 1:29,36).

The whole of the Old Testament traces the fulfillment of God's promise in Genesis 3:15 through Abraham's lineage. Then, at the start of Matthew's Gospel, we see it's a lineage that goes all the way to Jesus (Matt. 1:1-17). God had bigger plans for Abraham's faithful obedience than Abraham ever could have imagined. What a mile marker, a fingerprint of God's grace. The apostle Paul helps us understand this with his teaching in Galatians 3, which is about salvation through faith in Jesus, as compared to salvation by obedience to the Old Testament law.

So in Christ Jesus you are all children of God through faith, for all of you who were baptized into Christ have clothed yourselves with Christ. There is neither Jew nor Gentile, neither slave nor free, nor is there male and female, for you are all one in Christ Jesus. If you belong to Christ, then you are Abraham's seed, and heirs according to the promise.

GALATIANS 3:26-29

Abraham trusted God and He trusted God's plan. At other times in Genesis, Abraham walked in unfaithfulness. Praise God that we are not saved by our ability to keep God's law but rather by the perfect blood of Jesus that covers our weakness. Our hearts and our actions are littered with pride, selfishness, and self-preservation—rebellious postures against the Lord. But, Christ confirmed the Old Testament promises because His Word never fails (Romans 15:8). His promises never fail. In spite of our sin, God reigns true and calls His people to Himself.[10]

Bearing in mind what you have studied today, how do you see grace as a part of your everyday life? Where do you see evidence of it?

Moment by moment, generation to generation, God has kept His promises, and we get to build our faith on them today. A faith without wavering is one that is obedient out of response to God's grace. It's confident because it's seen God move. It's courageous because it knows who is with us in it all. You are called to live out obedience in the face of the unknown by following Jesus where *He* calls and where *He* leads. This week, ask God to help you be resilient in your obedience. With Jesus's death and resurrection behind you and the promise of His return ahead of you, walk in obedience today.

What next step of obedient faith is God calling you to take? What is holding you back?

Reflection

Often, we know the truths of obedience and grace in our heads, but they can be hard for us to embody in our hearts. Moving from head to heart is where our faith gets real. Ask yourself today: *Do I want a faith marked by long-suffering or shallowness? Do I want to follow Jesus or the idea of Him?* I want a relationship, not transactions. I want transformation, not information. I want to be marked by humility, not ability. Sacrifice, not selfishness. Grace, not guilt. Jesus, not me.

1. LOOK UP PSALM 145:13 AND 2 CORINTHIANS 1:20 and write them in the space below or on a separate note card. What is a truth that stands out to you as you read over these verses?

2. What is one big takeaway or main idea you want to remember from this week of study?

3. What is one idea or thought you need to lay down that contradicts God's faithful love for you?

4. Now, write out an honest prayer reflecting on the good news of the gospel, the surest sign of God's faithfulness to His promises, and the motivation for every obedient step we take in relationship with Him.

Video Viewer Guide

BUILDING RESILIENCE THROUGH FAITHFUL OBEDIENCE

WATCH the Session Five video and take notes below.

GROUP DISCUSSION / QUESTIONS FOR REFLECTION

A leader guide is available for download at lifeway.com/withoutwavering

1. What day of personal study had the most impact on you? Why?

2. How did what you heard on the video teaching clarify, reinforce, or give new insight into what you studied this session?

3. How were you encouraged by Abraham and Sarah's relationship with God as you studied them this week? How were you challenged?

4. One theme of Scripture is the cost, the sacrifice, that comes with a resilient, unwavering faith. As Alexandra noted in the video, "Obedience wouldn't be obedience without a cost." What is God calling you to sacrifice to follow Him today? Time? A relationship? A "want"? Discuss why sacrifice matters and why willingness is so hard.

5. Discuss your responses to the three reflection questions on page 108.

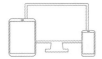

TO ACCESS THE VIDEO TEACHING SESSIONS, USE THE
INSTRUCTIONS IN THE BACK OF YOUR BIBLE STUDY BOOK.

109

Empty Doubt to
EMPOWERED FAITH

Over the last several weeks, we've considered how our faith grows through things like obedient living, spiritual rhythms, remembering God's promises and goodness, and His invitation to live by faith. This week, we're going to anchor ourselves in a handful of examples from Scripture whose stories inspire us to have a resilient faith. Their stories invite us to see what a life of unwavering faith in the character and promises of God can look like. As these friends in the faith encountered God, their confidence in Him grew, and they were able to face challenging, even traumatizing circumstances with confidence. This week my prayer for you is that you will be encouraged in God's power to do the same. We move from being victims of our circumstances to being overcomers in and through Jesus, the One who says, "Be courageous! I have conquered the world" (John 16:33b, CSB).

SESSION 06 MEMORY VERSE

I have told you these things so that in me you may have peace. You will have suffering in this world. Be courageous! I have conquered the world.

JOHN 16:33 (CSB)

RAHAB
Courageous Faith

I often look around and wonder how I got here. This faith of mine, the little I do have, wasn't built up overnight. It was fortified in the fire; it was tested and continues to be. I used to think I had more reason to doubt the goodness and faithfulness of God than to believe. The odds were stacked against me. Not to sound like a victim, but it was true. *Abuse, turmoil, dysfunction*—these were themes in my story. It has taken me a long time and a lot of wrestling to realize that God's love for me isn't about my circumstances, my strength, or my faith. It's about *His* being, *His* grace, *His* goodness.

I love the story of Rahab in the book of Joshua. This woman is not one to overlook. In fact, she's mentioned at pivotal moments in both the Old and New Testaments. Rahab has much to teach us about a courageous faith that's rooted in the character of God.

TAKE A FEW MOMENTS TO READ ALL OF JOSHUA 2. **As you read, write down key facts you learn about Rahab.**

After Moses died, Joshua became the leader of the Israelites and was in charge of leading them into the promised land (Josh. 1:6). The events of Joshua 2 describe their preparations for conquest. Joshua 2:1 introduces Rahab as "a prostitute named Rahab." Two Israelite spies took shelter in Rahab's house or inn. When the king of Jericho learned of the spies and sent a party to arrest them, Rahab hid the spies and threw off those who were looking for them.

REREAD JOSHUA 2:10-13. **What motivated Rahab to protect the spies?**

What did Rahab affirm about the God of Israel?

What stands out most to you about Rahab's message to the Israelite spies?

Rahab delivered a powerful message to the spies describing how her people had heard of the great victories of the Lord in leading His people out of slavery in Egypt and how their hearts melted with fear before the Israelites. One biblical scholar notes that this is "one of the longest uninterrupted statements by a woman in a biblical narrative."[1]

Being a Gentile woman and a Canaanite, she would not have had full details about the God of Israel, but she knew and gathered just enough.

VERSE 10 — Rahab knew of God's mighty deliverance of Israel out of Egypt.

VERSE 11 — She knew that judgment was coming and chose the right path to follow.

VERSE 11 — She knew the name of God, *Yahweh,* and that He is the God of heaven and earth.

VERSE 12 — She knew she wanted to find salvation for her family and herself.

I've searched and studied to see how this woman could have such a conviction to believe that this God was the God over all. But, alas, all I found is what is here. She simply chose to believe what she'd heard about the God of Israel. When she placed her faith in Him, God counted her among His people and saved her and her family from His wrath.

There's a beautiful gospel parallel happening in Rahab's story. For starters, *Joshua* and *Jesus* are the same name in Hebrew. Describe how you see Rahab's story pointing forward to Jesus.

Rahab's story reminds us of the good news of the gospel. Through faith in Jesus, we too join the family of God and are saved from His wrath. Rahab's story reminds us that Jesus saves, and any faith in Him is secure forever.

LOOK UP THE FOLLOWING PASSAGES OF SCRIPTURE. **Next to each reference below, note what additional details you learn about Rahab.**

Joshua 6:22-25

Matthew 1:5 and 1:16

Hebrews 11:31

James 2:25-26

For Rahab's courageous faith, for her yes in a moment when she could've easily said no, she is remembered among the faithful Old Testament heroes in the book of Hebrews.[2] The book of James points to Rahab as an example of someone whose faith in the one true God was lived out through her actions (Jas. 2:25).[3] Even though she did not know God well or know much about Him, she believed what she heard and trusted in Him, translating her faith into action. "Eventually, [Rahab] was no longer known as the harlot who hid the spies but as the wife of Salmon, the mother of Boaz, and the ancestor of Jesus (Matthew. 1:5-16)."[4]

So, what can we learn about our faith from Rahab? There are three takeaways I want to leave you with:

1. Faith in God moves us to action. We become people who live for Him and His purposes.

2. Our past does not disqualify us from living for and with God. No one is beyond the reach of His love and grace.

3. Third, our faithfulness and obedience can't be predicated on the opinions or decisions of others; it must be rooted in our confidence in Christ and His work alone.

Spend a few minutes reflecting on Rahab's story and the picture of the gospel you see in it. How does her example encourage and equip you to live with resilient faith?

Mary & Martha
ENDURING FAITH

It's one thing to have an unwavering faith when things are going well, or even when things are hard but bearable. But what about when we're up against the unbearable? What about in the face of grief and loss, when we look at the lack left behind and the overwhelming questions of *what's to come*? Where is faith in these moments?

I have faced trials that left me confused in my faith, wondering how on earth I was supposed to trust God again. I could tell you story after story of moments that seemed so dark and dreary, moments when there was no way light could have broken through. Wasn't Jesus supposed to be there? Wasn't He supposed to carry the heavier load (Matt. 11:28)? Wasn't He supposed to be enough? The sudden loss of my brother a few years ago left me stunned and thrown back into a world of family trauma and trials. And a few years before that we lost my father-in-law. Both losses unexpected, both full of anguish. And yet, my family endured, our faith endured, all because of Jesus.

The Gospel of John includes a story about Mary, Martha, and the death of their brother Lazarus that holds valuable insight for us on what it means to live from a place of enduring faith in the face of grief and tragedy. Let's look at it together.

> *OUR FAITH ENDURED, ALL BECAUSE OF JESUS.*

READ JOHN 11:1-15. **What stands out to you from the beginning of this story? What, if any, questions do you have?**

As I read through the beginning of this story, verses 13-15 stand out to me. Why would Jesus say He's glad He wasn't there when He knows He could have healed His friend? Instead of rushing to Lazarus's side, He waited two days. Mary and Martha were understandably confused, as you and I would be. Not only did Jesus tell

Lazarus's sisters not to worry about death, but He also said that Lazarus was asleep (v. 11). But also, I'll be there in two days; hang tight. Can you imagine?

Back in verse 4, Jesus made a small remark that's not to be missed: Jesus noted that Lazarus's sickness and the events that were about to unfold were a good thing: "It is for God's glory so that God's Son may be glorified through it." Jesus would make known His lordship even more, and people who saw would be moved to believe. He works things out for our good, growing our faith and forming our hearts, and ultimately giving all glory to God. "Lazarus' imminent death would give way to resurrection and the revelation of Jesus glorified as God's Son."[5]

The disciples' devotion to Jesus, along with the devotion of Mary and Martha, didn't mean they were enthusiastic about this decision to delay. We can't help but sympathize with Martha's response: "Lord . . . if you had been here, my brother would not have died" (v. 21). However, in a remarkable statement of faith in Jesus, she went on: "But I know that even now God will give you whatever you ask" (v. 22). Resilience doesn't spring up naturally or magically; it's built up in us over time and through endurance. Faith strengthens over time and often in the darkness and doubt of our trenches.

What follows in the next few verses is something I don't want us to miss. Jesus spoke words to Martha that gave her—and give us—a foundation to stand on in the midst of turmoil.

> READ JOHN 11:17-27. **Write down Jesus's "I am" statement in the space below (from v. 25).**

Jesus encouraged Martha in the face of her brother's death by referring to Himself as "the resurrection and the life"—"I am the resurrection and the life. The one who believes in me will live, even though they die; and whoever lives by believing in me will never die" (vv. 25-26). Jesus's life, death, and resurrection give us an eternal hope to stand on.

Now read the following list of the other "I am statements" from Jesus included in John's Gospel.

- I am the bread of life (John 6:35,48,51).

- I am the light of the world (John 8:12; 9:5).

- I am the door of the sheep (John 10:7,9).

- I am the good shepherd (John 10:11,14).

- I am the way, the truth, and the life (John 14:6).

- I am the true vine (John 15:1).

In summary, what do these verses teach you about Jesus and your relationship with Him? How do they help equip you in your faith?

The seven "I am" statements of Jesus are a central part of John's Gospel. God has always wanted us to know Him. These "I am" statements are not just descriptions of God but affirmations and reminders of His holy and righteous character. With every "I am" statement, Jesus affirmed His identity as the Messiah, the promised Redeemer foretold about in the Old Testament and the very Son of God. His desire for us to know and to see Him has always been. Even in Exodus 3:14, God identified Himself as "I AM WHO I AM." When we know who God is, we know why we can trust Him.

NOW LET'S READ JOHN 11:28-44 FOR THE REST OF THIS STORY.

Even as Jesus reminded His friends of His holiness and faithfulness, we also see that He grieved (v. 35). Although He knew that resurrection life was here, there was still a tension, a pain, a grieving that took place in the face of the harshest reality of our broken world. What a beautiful picture of both the heart of God for His children and also our ability to hold onto hope in the promises of God even while we lament.

Mary and Martha were met with a situation that seemed hopeless. And yet we see their faith grew stronger through trust and confidence in Jesus. When we know who controls it all, we are able to abide and rest in it all with Him. As we encounter hardships, God uses each moment to strengthen our faith in Him by building up our resilience, which then develops endurance.

Let's reframe our thinking some. Look at some moments of grief in your life. What do you see might have been an invitation to trust Jesus more in your situation?

How do you see God building in you a resilient, enduring faith in the current season of life you're in?

TESTED FAITH

Every time I had another loss, the wind would be kicked right out of me. With every hit, my desire to believe God and see God at work became thinner and thinner as the wall of what I thought was my rock-solid belief ended up being just one layer of thin, cheap Sheetrock®. One after another. Here came another betrayal. Another slight from the person at my job who relentlessly makes my life more difficult but so many miss. Everything felt unfair, and my faith stumbled.

One day I called one of my cousins while sitting in the Starbucks® drive-thru, a place where I find myself walking through so many of my conundrums. I shared how unfair I felt like life had been to me. How, unlike the choices of others that led to consequences and suffering and dismay, my sufferings didn't seem to be the result of my own doing. I strived to live from a place of genuine humility, willingness to obey, kindness, and overall pursuit of a lifestyle above reproach. I felt silly and embarrassed; my words surrounded me. I so often encourage others that if God allows something it will be for the good of our souls and His glory, but in that moment my heart revealed I didn't believe that. The heart so often needs reminding of the truth, doesn't it?

As much as I want to tell you that we aren't totally wrong for feeling hurt, anger, doubt, and even betrayal by God when life doesn't go our way, I can't. That couldn't be further from the truth.

Consider the story of Job, a man who experienced the loss of family, friends, belongings, and wealth, endured horrible illness that plagued him, and much more. The story starts off with the reality and teaching that God in fact had allowed these challenges to come Job's way.

READ JOB 1:1-12. **List the words/phrases that describe Job in the following verses.**

VERSE 1

VERSE 2

VERSE 3

According to verses 8-12, what was the spiritual framework for Job's intense suffering? Why did God permit it?

From the beginning of the book of Job, we learn he was a righteous man. The CSB translation describes him as a man of "complete integrity" (v. 1) He lived all the time the way we might hope to live on our best days. Through the glimpse we're given into God's conversation with Satan, we learn God permitted Satan to test Job by bringing immense trials into his life. One commentator notes, "Satan determined to prove that Job would not obey God if he got hardship in return. He claimed that selfishness prompted Job's obedience rather than love. Satan also believed that God would not get worship from Job if He stopped blessing him."[6] In reflecting on Job's response to his challenges, this commentator goes on to point out:

> Job grieved, but he also worshipped. These two activities are
> not incompatible. He saw God's hand in the events of his life.
> . . . Many people believe that if one has enough faith, he or she
> will always be happy. Job's experience does not bear this out.
> We should have a deep-seated joy no matter what happens to
> us, knowing that we are in the Lord's hands and that He has
> permitted whatever happens to us (Phil. 4:4). But we may not
> always be happy, namely, enjoying our circumstances.[7]

Job 1 takes us from hardship to hardship, from suffering to suffering, while we see Job trust God and believe, no matter what came his way. His faith was being tested in the fire, and we see that by faith he was resolved to believe in the God of ages, even when others questioned his journey. I place Job in the group of the faithful whom the writer of Hebrews referred to when he said, "And what more shall I say? . . . These were all commended for their faith, yet none of them received what had been promised" (Heb. 11:32,39).

Even though Job continued to believe in God, these years were a struggle for him, which chapters 2–37 make clear. (Read them when you have time!) When I read through his story though, I see two things I don't want us to miss as we consider Job's example of faithfulness—God's declaration of who He is and Job's unrelenting belief.

> READ JOB 38:1-7 AND JOB 42:1-6. **What can you learn from God's response to Job?**

What can you learn from Job's final words in the book?

OFTEN TRIALS, LOSS, AND PAIN ARE INGREDIENTS FOR THE GROWTH THAT DRAWS US CLOSER TO GOD AND HELPS US FEEL HIS LOVE AND GRACE MORE DEEPLY.

"God uses the example of Job to show that He will sometimes allow people to suffer even when they haven't done anything to 'deserve' the suffering."[8] It doesn't feel fair to call this love. And yet, often trials, loss, and pain are the ingredients for the growth that draws us closer to God and helps us feel His love and grace more deeply. These are moments that can lead to an unwavering faith in the One who still, even then, is holding it all together. And in it, we learn that we can endure because God is not only with us but for us.

If Job had known less suffering, He would've known less of the Lord. This goes for us as well.

Below are just a few verses in which Job responded to his suffering. Mark the one that speaks most strongly to you today.

☐ "The LORD gave, and the LORD has taken away; blessed be the name of the LORD" (Job 1:21b, ESV).

☐ "Though he [God] slay me, yet will I hope in him" (Job 13:15, NIV).

☐ "I know that my Redeemer lives, and he will stand upon the earth at last" (Job 19:25, NLT).

☐ I know that you can do anything and no plan of yours can be thwarted. You asked, "Who is this who conceals my counsel with ignorance?" Surely I spoke about things I did not understand, things too wondrous for me to know (Job 42:2-3, CSB).

God moved in Job's life to teach Him these truths, and through Jesus, these are truths we can claim, too. Slowly read the following passage from Romans and let Paul's words sink in:

> Therefore, since we have been justified by faith, we have peace with God through our Lord Jesus Christ. We have also obtained access through him by faith into this grace in which we stand, and we boast in the hope of the glory of God. And not only that, but we also boast in our afflictions, because we know that affliction produces endurance, endurance produces proven character, and proven character produces hope. This hope will not disappoint us, because God's love has been poured out in our hearts through the Holy Spirit who was given to us.
>
> ROMANS 5:1-5 (CSB)

NOW READ JAMES 5:11. **How did early Christians come to understand God better through Job's story?**

Our God is compassionate and merciful. Job knew these things to be true, and his story stands as a lasting example of God's character. Job's relationship with God made room for him to move through his suffering *with* God, taking every doubt and torment to Him. Today, you can take it all to Him, too. Honesty and grief open the door for God to move you into a faith empowered by Christ, knowing we can show up and give it all to Him. We press on toward the prize regardless of what's in front. We get back up, as we learn to run this race with endurance—toward Jesus, the Son of Righteousness, in all His majesty and beauty.

Samaritan Woman
FAITH THAT FUELS

Empty doubt. Those two words described me for a long time.

A few years ago, I found myself struck by the words of a father in the Gospel of Mark, a man who cried out to Jesus, "I do believe; help my unbelief!" (Mark 9:24). *A father, believing for a healing he couldn't yet see, hoping because of the Messiah he could see.* The encounter he had with Jesus left him different, in awe, in belief.

For me, this transition took time. I didn't fully grasp the depth of Jesus's sacrifice or my salvation in Him on the day I gave my life to Him. It took time; it developed in moments when my pride was stripped away, when I saw my lack, and as I grew to deeply understand Jesus's love for me. Unbelief turns to belief through a relationship with Jesus, and this is often a process.

> **When did the reality of God's mercy and grace begin to sink in for you? I mentioned how mine involved my pride being stripped away and seeing my lack. What is a word or phrase you would use to describe that shift in your life?**

John 4 has a story that may be familiar to you. It's the story of the Samaritan woman who met Jesus at a well. She is remembered largely for her controversial past, but that is such a small piece of this woman's story with Jesus. Today, we're going to dive a bit deeper into her encounter with Jesus and glean a more useful understanding of this moment in time. On an ordinary day, she made her way to the well where she meets Jesus, and the conversation between them left a new mark on her, a new identity. A holy exchange ensued, and her faith empowered her to tell others about Him.

READ JOHN 4:1-18. **Take note of any details you learn about the woman as you read.**

The woman at the well was a Samaritan, meaning she was a Gentile (not Jewish) from an enemy nation of Israel. She was also many times divorced. She carried shame attached to the reality that defined her; she was a woman who had been marked. However, Jesus went out of His way to make a way for her.[9]

For Jesus to be in Samaria at all was unusual, as Samaritans were considered unclean by the Israelites. It was doubly scandalous that He was talking to a woman. Racial division, gender taboos, and the class system would normally keep a man of Jesus's status from conversing with a woman such as her, much less drinking from her jar (John 4:7-9). And yet, Jesus leaned in. What He had to offer her—new life and a faith to stand on— was so much more important.

There are a few key moments in their conversation that I want us to focus on today.

1. JESUS SAVES US.

> Jesus said, "Everyone who drinks from this water will get thirsty again. But whoever drinks from the water that I will give him will never get thirsty again. In fact, the water I will give him will become a well of water springing up in him for eternal life." "Sir," the woman said to him, "give me this water so that I won't get thirsty and come here to draw water."
>
> JOHN 4:13-15 (CSB)

With these words, Jesus began to open the woman's eyes to who He is and why He was there. He wasn't there to get water from her; He was there to offer her "living water," a relationship with Him that would satisfy the thirst of her soul for eternity. "Jesus is talking about a new life that is available through the Spirit of God (4:14). . . . Christ himself is the source of precious living water, which can transform even this woman in her isolation. It is the 'gift' (*dorea*) of God—a word that later Christians associated with the Holy Spirit (Acts 2:38; 8:20; 10:45; 11:17; Heb. 6:4). But Jesus takes this promise a step further. It is not simply an experience that changes our 'state' (such as a 'state of salvation'), but it is a dynamic experience that makes a life as living as the water itself."[9]

2. JESUS KNOWS US AND REVEALS HIMSELF TO US.

> "Go call your husband," he told her, "and come back here." "I don't have a husband," she answered. "You have correctly said, 'I don't have a husband,'" Jesus said. "For you've had five husbands, and the man you now have is not your husband. What you have said is true."
>
> JOHN 4:16-18 (CSB)

> The woman said to him, "I know that the Messiah is coming" (who is called Christ). "When he comes, he will explain everything to us."
>
> JOHN 4:25 (CSB)

"Shocked by the truth of His words and exposure of her own sin, her eyes [began] to open to the truth of who [Jesus] is."[10] Through their conversation, He showed her His divine knowledge (Ps. 139) and affirmed His identity as the Messiah. In much the same way, we see clearly through Scripture who Jesus is and what He has done for us.

3. FAITH IN JESUS MOVES AND MOTIVATES US.

> Then the woman left her water jar, went into town, and told the people, "Come, see a man who told me everything I ever did. Could this be the Messiah?" They left the town and made their way to him.
>
> JOHN 4:28-30 (CSB)

The imagery of the abandoned water jar is powerful. The urgency of our sister moves me. Can you feel it? This new life she was offered changed everything for her. She met grace and hope. She met her Savior. I imagine Jesus here, overwhelmed with love for her. He showed her she mattered in the kingdom of God. Her life held a purpose and a mission. She left her water jar and ran to tell anyone she could about the God who saw all her wounds, her scars, her past and even present, and still offered her living water.

Take a minute to process these three statements: *Jesus changes us. Jesus knows us and reveals Himself to us. Faith in Jesus moves and motivates us.* **Which one did you most need to be reminded of today?**

BEFORE YOU WRAP UP, READ JOHN 4:39-42. **How did the woman's act of faith to tell her city about Jesus impact them?**

Who do you need to tell about the One who has transformed you, the One who has removed your sin and shame and given your life new purpose?

Faith is the evidence that there is a kind God we can trust in. The reminder of abundance where there seems to be lack. The supernatural work of the Spirit in us enables us to live with a faith that empowers others to see God and know God. May your faith in Christ spur you on.

day 05

Reflection

Think back on the stories you studied this week—Rahab, Mary and Martha, Job, and the Samaritan woman. Through these examples and so many more in God's Word, we learn what it looks like to move beyond doubt and fear from our circumstances to be women who live with a faith that is without wavering.

1. Whose story from this week's study revealed the most to you about your own relationship with God? What does a faith without wavering look like for you now as you reflect on these stories?

2. What is one big takeaway or main idea you want to remember from this week of study?

3. What is one idea or thought you need to lay down that contradicts God's faithful love for you?

4. Now write out an honest prayer of confession. Confess to God all the ways you try to live out of your own power rather than His. List specific examples from recent days. Confess the triggers that most often cause you to doubt His goodness and grace. Invite His Spirit to move in power in and through you today.

Video Viewer Guide

EMPTY DOUBT TO EMPOWERED FAITH

WATCH the Session Six video and take notes below.

GROUP DISCUSSION / QUESTIONS FOR REFLECTION

A leader guide is available for download at lifeway.com/withoutwavering

1. What day of personal study had the most impact on you? Why?

2. How did what you heard on the video teaching clarify, reinforce, or give new insight into what you studied this session?

3. We considered several more examples of unwavering faith this week. The more you've examined examples of faithfulness to God in Scripture and considered His faithfulness to you, how has your relationship with Him been impacted?

4. In this week's video teaching, Alexandra asked, "What have you placed your hope in? What is your faith fueled by?" How do you answer these questions today?

5. Discuss your responses to the three reflection questions on page 132.

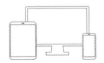

TO ACCESS THE VIDEO TEACHING SESSIONS, USE THE
INSTRUCTIONS IN THE BACK OF YOUR BIBLE STUDY BOOK.

Living with UNWAVERING FAITH

 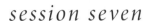

We've spent the last few weeks establishing ourselves in the gift that is an unwavering faith, a resilient one, built up, strengthened, and anchored in the promises of God. And now, we'll look at the ways in which having resilient faith informs our purpose, our character, and all the ways we live and love. When we live from a place of resilient faith, we become women equipped to take on the valleys of life and find hope, courage, strength, and joy in them.

My hope and prayer for you as you work through this final week of study is that God will move you from having faith to living out your faith, running the race God has set before you with endurance, courage, confidence, and renewed strength. It's time to conquer the mountains in life with faith fueled by Jesus's perseverance on the cross and the resilience that carried Him through.

SESSION 07 MEMORY VERSE

Let us hold on to the confession of our hope without wavering, since he who promised is faithful.

HEBREWS 10:23 (CSB)

LIVE BY *faith*

By faith.

We've talked a lot in this study about living "by faith" in the promises of God, and it's a beautiful concept—one I deeply desire for all of us. But those two little words can be so hard to hold onto. Our realities are hard, and no matter how much we want to live "by faith," some days we feel too tired or afraid to do so. What we do instead is hold our breath. We white-knuckle our way to the next season, the next move. We become angry and bitter. Instead of persevering in faith, we panic in fear. I've not had many moments in my life when I've displayed this "by faith" position well, but oh, how I desire for it to be my constant reality.

"I am tired of being tired." I uttered these words to my husband just a few months ago. I was sitting in my car with tears in my eyes. A lot happens in my car, maybe because it's where everything is so quiet I can hear God most clearly. I told Mario it was too hard to believe that better was coming when all I'd seen was hardship. And yet, as I worked on this study, as I examined the threads of resilience and perseverance in God's Word, I was reminded that living by faith is never about our push through the mud; it's about our positioning in Christ. This is what moves us to press on. Jesus gives us the strength and power to live resiliently by faith. We can have faith and still feel afraid, but faith won't keep us there; it moves us forward.

I've told you how much I like the apostle Paul. There's a moment in his ministry I want us to look at today because it gives us a great example of living by faith in Jesus.

> READ ACTS 18:1-8. **What was Paul doing in Corinth, and how did people respond to him?**

LOOK CLOSELY AT VERSE 6. What does the way Paul reacted to opposition teach you about your purpose and your faith?

Paul, committed to the preaching and teaching of the gospel, was kicked out of the synagogue by the Jews. They were angry and hurtful toward Paul because of the words he spoke about Jesus. If you look back in Acts through Paul's previous missionary work, you'll see this type of opposition wasn't new for him. He had already endured much for the sake of the gospel, yet he remained faithful to the work God called him to do.[1]

I can only imagine how physically and emotionally exhausted Paul must have been, but the prize—drawing people to Jesus—was worth the cost. And look at how God encouraged him:

> One night the Lord spoke to Paul in a vision: "Do not be afraid; keep on speaking, do not be silent. For I am with you, and no one is going to attack and harm you, because I have many people in this city."
>
> ACTS 18:9-10

"For I am with you."

Paul's commitment to live for Christ was fueled by God's promise to be with Him, and ours should be too. The comfort we find in the Father's arms is even more overwhelming than our circumstances. Not only did Jesus's words to Paul encourage him, but they moved him to persevere, to actively rest in Jesus while living out the call set before him. The text goes on to tell us Paul stayed committed to his work in Corinth for a year and a half (v. 11), and we know he wrote at least two letters to the church there after he moved on (1 & 2 Cor.).

What is a situation in which you need to be reminded of God's promise to be with you? When you take that to heart, how does it reframe what you're going through?

The promise of God's presence with us is life-changing in so many ways. Here are a few in particular:

1. We don't need to live in fear (Isa. 41:10).

2. Our lives are a testimony that draws others to Christ (Rom. 10:17).

3. We can rest assured that God will never leave us or forsake us (Deut. 31:8).

4. We are empowered to live out the work God has given us to do (Matt. 28:20).

God's presence is our daily bread, manna, and provision in all we lack. I love this encouragement from King David in Psalm 27:

> The LORD is my light and my salvation; whom shall I fear? The LORD is the stronghold of my life; of whom shall I be afraid? When evildoers assail me to eat up my flesh, my adversaries and foes, it is they who stumble and fall. Though an army encamp against me, my heart shall not fear; though war arise against me, yet I will be confident.
>
> PSALM 27:1-3 (ESV)

God's challenge to Paul was to keep going, to get back up. To follow Jesus is to live a life marked by long-suffering love and holy perseverance.

What have you been living by? Fear? Acceptance? Knowledge? Control? Take a minute to consider your response.

Now, ask Jesus to exchange your tiredness for His strength, your lack for His abundance. Write out a prayer of surrender to Him, and then sit quietly in His presence.

BE ROOTED
in Jesus

There's a lake I like to go to about an hour from our house. It's one of the first bodies of water close enough to drive to that I got to experience with my oldest girl. I would take her on walks in her stroller around the lake all the time. Her little feet dangling over the seat, her big brown eyes full of wonder and awe. I love masses of water and wanted her to feel the love and peace there as I do. Creation draws me near to God like your favorite instrumental piano and guitar music might—melodic, emotional, dreamy, and bright. Every beautiful note pointing to the glory of the Creator.

Safety. The feeling of being grounded. A settling of the soul.

This feeling is the settling we are invited into when trusting Jesus in it all. Thinking back to yesterday's study, I imagine this is how Paul felt and wanted others to feel—at home with God and empowered in Him.

> **Do you have a place you go to that settles your soul? That reminds you of God's power in you? It may not be a place like the lake I visit, but maybe it's a Bible verse you take refuge in, or an activity you like to do. If so, what is it, and how does it help you rest in God's presence?**

We began our study in the book of Hebrews, and I want us to end there, too.

<u>READ HEBREWS 10:19-22, PRINTED HERE.</u>

> [19] Therefore, brothers and sisters, since we have confidence
> to enter the Most Holy Place by the blood of Jesus, [20] by
> a new and living way opened for us through the curtain,
> that is, his body, [21] and since we have a great priest over
> the house of God, [22] let us draw near to God with a sincere
> heart and with the full assurance that faith brings, having
> our hearts sprinkled to cleanse us from a guilty conscience
> and having our bodies washed with pure water.

Underline the statement in these verses that sums up what our faith, our confidence, is rooted in.

Now, write your own paraphrase of verse 19. Make this your declaration of unwavering faith in the Lord.

WE STAND ON THE POWER OF JESUS.

We stand on the power of Jesus. Instead of having to wait until eternity to stand in the presence of God or be dependent on a human priest to do the work for us, we live in His presence today. We stand in "full assurance" of faith because of the forgiveness, grace, and life available to us through Jesus. When we stand in the confidence we have in Jesus, our faith is unshakeable. Imagine being able to carry that feeling with you, that confidence of safety knowing all will be right in the end. You can, and that's incredible! Jesus gives us this gift.

But the Counselor, the Holy Spirit, whom the Father will send in my name, will teach you all things and remind you of everything I have told you. Peace I leave with you. My peace I give to you. I do not give to you as the world gives. Don't let your heart be troubled or fearful.

JOHN 14:26-27 (CSB)

Do you not know that your bodies are temples of the Holy Spirit, who is in you, whom you have received from God? You are not your own.

1 CORINTHIANS 6:19 (NIV)

For we are the temple of the living God. As God has said: "I will live with them and walk among them, and I will be their God, and they will be my people."

2 CORINTHIANS 6:16b (NIV)

These verses are a sweet reminder for our hearts and minds. Read them again. What do you think it looks like to live out the truth in these verses, to walk through your day as someone who has the Spirit of God dwelling in her?

We are temples of the living God, which means He truly is with us always. Everything about us—who we are and how we live—should be a reflection of this profound truth. Jesus's peace proclaims goodwill on earth, and the presence of the Spirit with us leaves no room for angst or fear. I want you to find rest in these truths.[2]

Before you wrap up your study time today, I want to encourage you with a few more verses. Pick one of these verses to memorize. Write it on a piece of paper to carry with you or stick on your mirror, or make it the wallpaper on your phone so you see it often.

You reveal the path of life to me; in your presence is abundant joy; at your right hand are eternal pleasures.

PSALM 16:11 (CSB)

Brothers and sisters, I do not consider myself to have taken hold of it. But one thing I do: Forgetting what is behind and reaching forward to what is ahead, I pursue as my goal the prize promised by God's heavenly call in Christ Jesus.

PHILIPPIANS 3:13-14 (CSB)

We are hard-pressed on every side, but not crushed; perplexed, but not in despair; persecuted, but not abandoned; struck down, but not destroyed.

2 CORINTHIANS 4:8-9 (NIV)

Like Paul in Philippians 3, we live with a resilient faith by simply taking the next step forward as those who are anchored in Christ's firm foundation. We may come against some resistance, but we know who is with us and who we are rooted in. No matter what may come, we remain in Him.

HOLD ON
to Hope

As I've grown in my understanding of who God is and who I am as His daughter, I've come to see hope much differently. The hope that's easy to grab hold of is the hope that good things are coming your way, that you'll make it through the next valley, jump the next hurdle, or overcome the next challenge. I grabbed on to this kind of hope for years only to have it slip through my fingers like sand with every new hardship I faced.

The hope God desires for us to have in Him is different. This hope is concrete; it is certain and unwavering because it is rooted in the faithful One. The Bible verse that inspired the title of this study is Hebrews 10:23, "Let us *hold on to the confession of our hope without wavering*, since he who promised is faithful" (CSB, emphasis added). When our faith is firmly attached to the hope we have in Jesus and the promise of His return, we become women who view our days as opportunities rather than obstacles, as the chance to live for God and bring glory to His name.

Can you think of a time when your hope in Jesus carried you through? How do you think you would have felt in that same season without Jesus?

REREAD HEBREWS 10:19-22 FROM YESTERDAY'S STUDY.

Now, consider the next statement the writer of Hebrews made:

Let us hold on to the confession of our hope without wavering, since he who promised is faithful.

HEBREWS 10:23 (CSB)

In your own words, what is "the confession of our hope"?

The original recipients of Hebrews included Jewish Christians who may have been tempted to return to Judaism if or when they faced persecution for being Christians. The writer wanted to make sure they understood just how much their lives were changed because of Jesus (see 10:1-18) and the hope they had in Him.

One Bible commentary notes the following in response to Hebrews 10:23,

> The complete salvation for which we wait will arrive when Jesus reappears from heaven (9:28). In the meantime our hope is sustained by the assurance that God, who promised us rescue and rest, "is faithful." He has sealed his promises by two unchangeable things in which he cannot lie: his promise to Abraham and his oath sworn to Christ as a priest forever after the order of Melchizedek (6:12–18). Therefore we, like ancient believers such as Sarah (11:11), can rely on his faithfulness.[3]

THE HOPE GOD DESIRES FOR US TO HAVE IN HIM IS CERTAIN AND UNWAVERING.

Living with unwavering faith means we make an effort to remember—actively call to mind and cling to—the promises of God and the hope we have in Him.

> Thus says the LORD: "Cursed is the man who trusts
> in man and makes flesh his strength, whose heart
> turns away from the LORD. He is like a shrub in the
> desert, and shall not see any good come. He shall
> dwell in the parched places of the wilderness, in
> an uninhabited salt land. "Blessed is the man who
> trusts in the LORD, whose trust is the LORD. He is
> like a tree planted by water, that sends out its roots
> by the stream, and does not fear when heat comes,
> for its leaves remain green, and is not anxious in the
> year of drought, for it does not cease to bear fruit."
>
> JEREMIAH 17:5-8 (ESV)

What do these verses help you better understand about faith through the nature imagery?

When we look back at where God has brought us, when we see how far we've come; when we remember, renewed hope rises up in us. We remember the work of Christ and the faithfulness of the cross. Remember, this isn't blind faith; it's a steady and proven one.

> Just as people are destined to die once, and after
> that to face judgment, so Christ was sacrificed
> once to take away the sins of many; and he will
> appear a second time, not to bear sin, but to bring
> salvation to those who are waiting for him.
>
> HEBREWS 9:27-28

We all want the easy way out of the hard things. But in God's upside-down kingdom, it's in and through the wilderness and fire that we build up a faith that is without wavering. What better testimony than to let our resilient faith tell the world of this great love that has been poured out for them. (More on that tomorrow!) For today, sit with the words of God you've read, and let them stir up in you a sturdier hope.

Reflect on the ways God has met you in hardship and suffering. What test and trial has He transformed into a memory of His faithful and steadfast love? What testimony has He invited you into?

Spend a few minutes in reflective prayer. Consider your responses to those last questions. Praise God for who He is and the promises He's given you to hold onto. Then, close by praying this personalized version of Hebrews 10:23 aloud:

Let me hold on to the confession of my hope without wavering since You are faithful.

Go Out;
DON'T MISS OUT

There comes a time early in your walk with God when you make an active choice to believe that what you know about God is true. This moment—the moment when you become not just aware of God's splendor, but in awe of it—is when the roots of your faith are strengthened, when you are drawn out.

I have a very vivid memory of sitting in a coffee shop reading through 2 Corinthians and feeling a great sense of excitement and expectancy about life. I was maybe three years into my relationship with Jesus—three years of getting to know and see what grace was all about. I remember sitting there, looking around at all the people and wondering if, like me before I met Jesus, maybe they just didn't know there was more to life. Looking back, I think that day was the day I decided to let faith flow through me. To not let the fear of the unknown deter me from what I knew to be true. And to not shy away from telling others this unimaginably good news.

Yesterday, we considered Hebrews 10:23 and its call to persevere in the hope of God's faithfulness. But, as always, there's more to the verses we've been gifted to steward.

READ HEBREWS 10:23-25. **What additional instruction did the writer of Hebrews give readers in verses 24-25? (Hint: Pay close attention to the verbs in these verses!)**

Following the writer's appeal to "hold onto the confession of our hope without wavering," he gave readers these words:

> And let us consider how to spur one another
> on to love and good deeds. Let us not neglect
> meeting together, as some have made a habit,
> but let us encourage one another, and all the
> more as you see the Day approaching.
>
> HEBREWS 10:24-25 (BSB)

The original readers, like us, were likely discouraged, maybe even disillusioned, because of the things life was throwing their way, especially what they faced because of their belief in Jesus. And yet they, also like us, were given the call to encourage one another and share about their faithful God with others because this would be the clear and comforting news their souls needed.

Don't hold back on sharing your faith and meeting together (v. 25). In other words, don't keep this hope to yourselves. Instead, "spur one another on to love and good deeds" (v. 24, BSB) and "encourage one another" (v. 25, BSB). A faith without wavering is one that focuses outward. It's one that is relentless in its effort to reach others with the hope of glory. God calls us to join Him in His mission to reach the world with the good news about Jesus.

READ MATTHEW 28:16-20. Summarize your mission as a follower of Jesus according to verses 18-20.

Think back on what you've learned about faith through our study. How does a resilient faith better equip you to live out God's mission?

Some will doubt your authenticity as they see your faith grow strong and as you testify to it. How can you walk with those who may not see it yet? If you have a person in mind, what are some specific ways you can encourage and walk alongside that person?

God's commission to His family has always been to go and tell about this hope we know to be true.[4] We are to live a life that is the aroma of Christ to those around us (2 Cor. 2:15). And so, we go. We tell others about the hope of Jesus and testify to the faith we know to be true and good. And we encourage others who are doing the same.

I hope as you've walked through this study you've learned that faith isn't about seeing or feeling but trusting and believing—believing in the character and promises of our ever-faithful God.

> *May the truths you've learned from God's Word ring true for years to come for you. May you cherish them in your mind and hide them in your heart.*
>
> *May you be inspired by the faith of Abraham and Sarah, Rahab, Paul, Martha, and so many others.*
>
> *May you look back at Job and learn to model his patience and long-suffering.*
>
> *May you feel the Lord's power in and through your life.*
>
> *May each storm be seen as a place of worship.*
>
> *May you get back up in Christ after each wave crashes over you.*
>
> *May Christ Jesus build up in you a resilient faith that is without wavering—built not on sandcastles but on the cornerstone (Eph. 2:20).*

Reflection

I can't believe that this is your last reflection day! I'm so proud of you and the work you've put into studying God's Word over the past six weeks. I hope and pray you've grown in your understanding of who God is and you've learned to trust Him more. And I pray that as your relationship with Jesus grows, so does your desire to tell others about Him.

1. How do you feel as you reach the end of this study? What have you learned about the character of God? What do you understand about faith that you didn't before this study? Whom do you need to tell about the hope you have in Jesus?

2. What is one big takeaway or main idea you want to remember from this week of study?

3. What is one idea or thought you need to lay down that contradicts God's faithful love for you?

4. Now write out a prayer of praise. Begin your prayer with these words from Paul: "Now to him who is able to do above and beyond all that we ask or think according to the power that works in us—to him be glory in the church and in Christ Jesus to all generations, forever and ever" (Eph. 3:20-21, CSB).

Video Viewer Guide

LIVING WITH UNWAVERING FAITH

WATCH the Session Seven video and take notes below.

GROUP DISCUSSION / QUESTIONS FOR REFLECTION

A leader guide is available for download at lifeway.com/withoutwavering

1. What day of personal study had the most impact on you? Why?

2. How did what you heard on the video teaching clarify, reinforce, or give new insight into what you studied this session?

3. One of the important truths in this last session of study is the reminder that faith is a gift from God that we use to glorify Him and help grow His kingdom. Who needs to see your faith in action today? Who needs to know the good and faithful God you serve? How can your group hold one another accountable?

4. Toward the end of this session's teaching, Alexandra asked, "What makes for a faith that's without wavering?" How would you answer that question today, at the end of your study?

5. Discuss your responses to the three reflection questions on page 153.

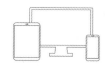

TO ACCESS THE VIDEO TEACHING SESSIONS, USE THE
INSTRUCTIONS IN THE BACK OF YOUR BIBLE STUDY BOOK.